Some Like It Hot

SOME LIKE IT HOT
FLOWERS
THAT THRIVE IN HOT HUMID WEATHER

P.J. GARTIN

Wyrick & Company

AN IMPRINT OF GIBBS SMITH, PUBLISHER

Salt Lake City | Charleston | Santa Fe | Santa Barbara

Other titles by P.J. Gartin
Some Like It Hot: Plants That Thrive in Hot and Humid Climates
(with F. Brian Smith)

First Edition
11 10 09 08 07   5 4 3 2 1

Published by
Wyrick & Company
An imprint of Gibbs Smith, Publisher
P.O. Box 667
Layton, Utah 84041

Orders: 1.800.835.4993
www.gibbs-smith.com

Cover designed by Leticia Le Bleu
Interior designed by Sally Heineman
Printed and bound in Hong Kong

 Library of Congress Cataloging-in-Publication Data

Gartin, P. J.
  Some like it hot : flowers that thrive in hot humid weather / PJ Gartin.
— 1st ed.
      p. cm.
  Includes bibliographical references and index.
  ISBN-13: 978-0-941711-91-3 (alk. paper)
  ISBN-10: 0-941711-91-9 (alk. paper)
  1. Gardening. 2. Flowers—Southern States. 3. Gardening—Southern
States. 4. Plants, Ornamental—Southern States. I. Title.
  SB407.G348 2007
  635.9'52--dc22
                        2006031240

Contents

Foreword

This book is for every southern gardener who has ever plotted, planned, or dreamed about keeping summertime annuals and perennials alive and blooming throughout the endless days of scorching temperatures and relentlessly high humidity. Home gardening always looks so simple and effortless in mid-January when the spring catalogs begin to arrive and all those adorable plants shout, "Buy me!" from every page. What fun it is to fantasize about hundreds of square feet filled with colorful, continually blooming, pest-free flowers. Who cares if the last frost date is still a good six weeks away and we don't have an extra hundred square feet to our name?

Acknowledgments

Writing a gardening book is a lot like playing in a string quartet or running in a road race. Although they can be intensely personal and sometimes deeply lonely, no one can get through such affairs by themselves. The camaraderie and support that comes with writing a book is much like a convivial evening spent with friends to play a couple of Mozart quartets or waiting with your pals for the starting gun to go off. I could have never completed this book without my friends' and associates' unfailing support.

Many thanks to chemist Chris Woolhouse for providing the technical information on how *Hibiscus mutabilis* changes color and to computer scientist Dr. Jimmy Wilkinson for keeping my computer from crashing. I am indebted to my former editor and now good friend, Laura Moses, for braving an early morning, bone-chilling photo shoot at Charleston's Waterfront Park for me. I am also grateful to my longtime confidant Lynn Katz Danzig for her professional photography advice and gentle instruction. I wish to thank Dr. Richard Porcher for graciously offering to share his botanical photograph library and I would also like to thank Dr. Michael Hull for giving me Louisa Cameron's photographs of his private garden.

I send a big Texas thanks to my sister, Cathi Lane, co-owner of Sandyhill Plant Farm in Mineola. I deeply appreciate her horticultural knowledge and photography skills. And to my former co-author F. Brian Smith, who has moved on to another profession, thank you for a terrific journey.

I extend my thanks to the Charleston County Clemson Extension Service Master Gardeners, as well as to the Master Gardeners in Wilmington, North Carolina. I am also indebted to the cooperative extension services at Auburn University, Clemson University, Louisiana State University, North Carolina State University, Texas A & M University, University of Florida, University of Georgia, and Virginia Polytechnic Institute and State University. And I will be forever grateful to Dr. Edward F. Gilman, University of Florida Cooperative Extension Service, who is one of the southeast's most knowledgeable and prolific horticulture writers.

I would also like to thank Tony Avent, owner of Plant Delights Nursery and Juniper Level Botanical Gardens in Raleigh, North Carolina, who not only opened up his fabulous property to fellow members of the Garden Writers Association last summer, but unselfishly shares his plant wisdom with all. I am also indebted to Cross Seed Company's plant specialist Leslie Wampler and store manager Mark VanHouten for graciously allowing me to take photographs.

I am most certainly beholden to the renowned horticulturist and educator Dr. Allan M. Armitage, as well as to Dr. Marc Cathey, President Emeritus of the American Horticultural Society. I am also obliged to Ramon Jordan, Research Plant Pathologist at the U. S. National Arboretum, David J. Ellis, editor of the American Horticultural Society's *The American Gardener*, and for the professional counsel of John W. Hazard, Jr. I am grateful for the opportunity to use the many data bases provided by the United States Department of Agriculture and the National Oceanic and Atmospheric Administration. I acknowledge Thompson & Morgan for making their always reliable, seed-growing information available to home gardeners and to W. Atlee Burpee & Company and George W. Park Seed Company, Inc.

One of the most enjoyable things about Charleston is the abundance of libraries. I could not have written this book without the aid of the Charleston Library Society, The Citadel's Daniel Library, and the Charleston County Public Library. I am indebted to countless staff members, many of whom have become my friends.

I extend sincere thanks to my stoic publisher/editor Pete Wyrick, to my talented book designer Sally Heineman, and to my wonderful literary friends and confidants, Susan Day and Marcia Miles. But most of all, I want to thank my husband, John C. Bernens, for his unfaltering belief in me. This is a man who has patiently listened to hundreds of renditions of *Eine Kleine Nachtmusik*, who always gets up before dawn to send me off to a race, who has read and edited thousands of my words, and has never kept me from doing what makes me happy.

Introduction

There have probably been millions of pages written about growing plants in hot weather. However, not many address the peculiarities of hot and humid gardening, especially when it comes to herbaceous plants. I suspect that part of this is because it can be treacherous territory.

There are fewer horticultural absolutes when it comes to growing annuals and perennials than with woody ornamentals. We also seem to expect more out of the smaller plants than the big guys. Why is it that we will patiently wait for a year or two before giving up on an expensive, medium-sized shrub, but go to pieces over a three-dollar annual that was impulsively purchased at the grocery store? Under such circumstances, some may find offering recommendations for hot and humid gardens a bit daunting.

For those who are familiar with *Some Like It Hot: Plants That Thrive in Hot and Humid Weather*, you might be surprised to learn that I'm simply mad about annuals and perennials. After all, my co-author, F. Brian Smith, and I insisted that we find most herbaceous annuals (except for vines) to be a nuisance. And, we said, "It seems to us that many annuals are just too seasonally specific." Have I changed my mind or were Brian and I just pulling that old sophomoric poetic license routine? The truth is, there are plenty of wonderful annuals, as well as perennials, that will flourish in extreme heat and humidity. The challenge is discovering which plants will work in specific situations. And because herbaceous plants have tender stems instead of woody ones, they can be more difficult or temperamental to grow than shrubs.

Even experienced gardeners know that selecting the right annuals and perennials for warm weather enjoyment can quickly add up to nothing but frustration. If you have ever knocked yourself silly planting carefully selected flowering plants, only to spend the rest of the summer agonizing over their survival, then you probably live below the Mason-Dixon Line.

Gardening in Dixie sometimes requires us to ask horticultural, even botanical, questions that would never be thought of in cooler climates. Sometimes asking technical questions is difficult because we don't all speak the same language. It has been my experience that one of the biggest obstacles to gardening in the Deep South is our American ability to ignore botanical nomenclature. We can collectively have five different names for some cherished flower, yet few of us know its scientific name. It's hard to intelligently discuss specific horticultural requirements when none of us are sure what we're talking about. Yes, calling plants by their Latin names can sound pretentious (and that *is* why some do it), but it's a universal language and a powerful gardening tool.

I've been tending the same garden in Charleston, South Carolina, since 1987. It should, therefore, come as no surprise to other seasoned gardeners that I have also cultivated some biases along the way. But being a Clemson Extension Service Master Gardener volunteer has afforded me not only a greater perspective on the fine art of Deep South gardening, but an awareness of our differences in horticultural tastes and interests.

For example, while some of us in USDA Hardiness Zones 8b–11 would cringe at the thought of allowing *Lantana camera* in our gardens, folks further up the road in North Carolina are clamoring for lantana new varieties that will survive Hardiness Zone 7 winters. Others consider *verbena rigida* mere weeds, while some gardeners purchase its seed and turn it loose in their gardens. Although we may never agree upon our likes and dislikes, I have attempted to offer a broad selection of annuals and perennials, plus a few other interesting, but not quite herbaceous, ones, that are suitable for a summertime

Lantana
Lantana camera

Verbena
Verbena rigida

southeastern garden. My list is hardly all-inclusive and I never intended it to be. I tried to eliminate plants that flop, because tying and staking during the sweltering heat of summer is not fun. While very few plants for southern gardens are completely pest free, my assortment should fare better than others. Since I despise that scourge of the south, powdery mildew, I have given readers a heads-up if this might be a threat to a particular plant. Naturally, a lot of my selections are based upon my own gardening adventures. However, before a particular species could make it to my final list, our southeastern land grant schools also had to recommend it.

Invasiveness: When Plants Become More Than Pests

The fascinating, yet also frustrating, truth about gardening is the abundance of horticultural ambiguities. Even when we sincerely believe that we are relying on scientifically proven practices, something eventually comes along and challenges our perceptions, beliefs, or habits. And no matter how hard we try to remain objective about a thought-provoking situation, our first reaction is often an emotional one.

The subject of invasive plants has become important not only to environmentalists but also to gardeners. However, we have collectively had problems when it comes to defining the word *invasive*. As a result, this issue can sometimes turn into an emotional topic.

Mention *Lantana camera* to someone who lives in Florida and their reaction to this plant will be quite negative. This species of lantana is from the West Indies but has made itself too much at home. The Florida Exotic Pest Plant Council considers it to be invasive. This plant can grow to over 6 feet tall in the Sunshine State and reproduces in abundance from seed. Yet, the *L. camera* that has been growing in my garden for at least a couple of decades has never made it to 5 feet tall and I have never plucked out new seedlings. I have seen what I suspect are volunteers growing in Charleston, but I have never seen them in profusion. Are we doing something horticulturally incorrect because our friends in Florida are fighting to control *L. camera* and we continue to grow it?

Perhaps we should follow the I'll-know-it's-invasive-when-I-see-it Rule. After all, no one is going to defend the merits of kudzu or hydrilla. They are clearly obnoxious to everyone. But how should we treat other plants? Where do we draw the line?

Some of my plant recommendations in this book might be considered—if not invasive—certainly undesirable for some situations. In those instances, I have included caveats about potentially bad behaviors.

Plant Selection Criteria

Before my co-author, F. Brian Smith, and I began writing *Some Like It Hot: Plants That Thrive in Hot and Humid Weather*, we devised a criteria for what makes a plant a "some-like-it-hot" one. Although that book covered trees, shrubs, ornamental grasses, and annual vines, we agreed that our plants should offer robust bloom, vibrant berries, interesting bark, or, at the very least, display exceptional leaf color during the height of a southeastern summer. I have used many of the same standards for annuals and perennials when applicable.

Of course, expecting the same kind of summertime resilience from herbaceous plants is a rather tall order when comparing them to their larger cousins. Annuals and perennials usually need more attention than woodies, and sometimes we must spend several hot months fussing over a species that won't reward us with spectacular bloom until the end of summer. Chrysanthemums first come to mind, and I would be remiss if they were not included in this book.

Many of my recommendations come from my own gardening experiences and observations. As a Clemson Extension Service Master Gardener, I have also learned how to grow many varieties of annuals and perennials that will never take up residence in my own garden. And like everyone else who has ever held a handful of soil, I have craved what I cannot or probably won't ever have. These often turn out to be the plants that we love to learn about and end up knowing more about than some of the ones that we regularly tend. They are just too irresistible not to write about.

My plant selections had to successfully grow in all types of hot and humid gardens. If I had any doubts or questions about their performance, I consulted our land grant schools' horticulture departments for verification, as well as additional information. Of course, it shouldn't surprise anyone in the green industry that not all schools agree on everything. If there were slight horticultural disagreements, spelling discrepancies, or botanical names differed, I deferred to Allan Armitage.

I also took into consideration that, while some southeastern gardeners are

'Profusion' Beautyberry
Callicarpa bodinieri
'Profusion'

continually demanding new kinds of annuals and perennials, others are still trying to figure out how to grow old standards. I have tried to satisfy both camps.

The Difference Between Herbaceous and Woody Plants

Some say that the distinction is quite simple: There are shrubs and there are flowers. But, then, what is my *Lantana camera*? Like my butterfly bush (*Buddleia davidii*), which is a woody ornamental, the lantana also flowers throughout the summer. Yet it is as big and as "shrubby" as the butterfly bush. The answer lies in their stems.

Herbaceous plants are usually not as robust as woodies because woodlike stems are obviously tougher than tender, green ones. Some woody ornamentals such as gardenia, azalea (*Rhododendron* spp.), and hollies (*Ilex* spp.) keep their green leaves all year round. Others, such as butterfly bush (*B. davidii*) and beautyberries (*Callicarpa* spp.) lose their leaves in winter and send out new ones in the spring. On the other hand, herbaceous plants such as perennials die to the ground after a frost then spend most of the winter in dormancy. In late winter or early spring, they send out new growth and their life cycle begins again. Of course, annuals are also herbaceous plants but they will not survive freezing temperatures.

I must warn you, however, that I have expanded my flower selections beyond what most gardeners think of as strictly annuals and perennials. Some of my plants, such as the Confederate rose (*Hibiscus mutabilis*) might even be considered a tree in some situations.

Confederate rose
Hibiscus mutabilis

Our Southern Signature: Heat and Humidity

Whenever southern gardeners are told that a desirable plant does well in hot weather, most of us are eager to try it. However, in our fit of horticultural excitement we often forget to ask if this marvelous plant will also survive our crushing summertime humidity.

Whenever southern gardeners are told that a desirable plant does well in hot weather, most of us are eager to try it. However, in our fit of horticultural excitement we often forget to ask if this marvelous plant will also survive our crushing summertime humidity. And this is where we get ourselves into trouble. From my own gardening experiences, I have learned that many gardening disappointments result from either incomplete growing information or our own misguided expectations about a plant's performance in hot and humid weather.

But why is this humidity issue so important? Isn't it the *heat* that melted our once thriving, herbaceous border? After all, the humidity hardly disappears during our mostly mild Deep South winters. If it doesn't seem to be a factor in winter, then what makes it so important in the summertime?

Heat and humidity make a dangerous team

I am almost as devoted to the sport of running as I am to gardening. For the past several years, I have faithfully run the streets of Charleston, usually five days a week, every week of the year. Although a discussion of my favorite sport may seem like a strange subject for a gardening book, there are stunning scientific similarities between plant and human heat stress. Since most of us can probably recall what it feels like to be hot and winded after strenuous activity, it should be fairly easy to identify with heat-stressed plants. At the risk of anthropomorphizing, we should at least empathize with their pain. A lot of our favorite plant buddies don't like the heat and humidity any more than we do.

During the summer months, our physical discomfort, whether we're running, gardening, or blooming, can be squarely blamed on the Deep South's meteorological scourge: the heat and its always present companion, invisible vaporized water.

When we refer to relative humidity, we are talking about the percentage of water that ambient air can hold at a particular temperature. And wouldn't you know it? Warm air can hold more water vapor than cold air. When I went out for a run at seven o'clock one morning, it was 81 degrees. The relative humidity was 94 percent and I felt like I was trapped inside a plastic bag. Running in that kind of "soup" meant that my chances of being swacked by heat stress were much greater than if I had run those same 4 miles in 90-degree weather in the arid southwest. This is because moisture-saturated air prevents perspiration from evaporating.

Anyone who remembers a speck of junior high science knows that evaporation has a cooling effect. But when the relative humidity goes up, the vapor pressure gradient between the ambient air and damp surfaces is reduced. In other words, we become miserably hot and sticky when we can't get rid of our perspiration. Although plants don't exactly perspire, they stay cool by moving water up through their roots and stems and then transpiring it through their leaves. But when the relative humidity gets too high for some of them, their transpiration rate slows down because there's no room left in the air to shed their excess moisture. Just like us, they begin to "feel" lousy so they begin physically fighting to cool off. But if these perilous conditions occur every summer, how does anyone or anything survive the heat and humidity?

A plant's chances for surviving hot and humid situations depend on its genetic predisposition, but environmental conditions such as light and wind are also important variables. Gardeners can improve their plants' chance of survival by simply thinking about how we humans readjust our routines to get through the summer. It's called acclimatization. In other words, we gradually make physical adjustments to new environmental conditions.

If you live in the sultry south, you know that one can become accustomed to almost any kind of sticky heat. After all, some folks work outdoors for a living, and no one shuts down the construction or landscaping business from June to September just because it gets too hot. Like everyone else, I go through about a week of complaining, followed by a few bouts of honest sulking, before I finally surrender to the realities of summer. We all drink more water and learn to slow down. Runners decrease their mileage on the hottest of days and even grudgingly break into walks now and then. Sensible gardeners plan their chores around the cooler parts of hot and muggy days. If we didn't, we'd last about as long as our cool-season garden favorites at the beginning of June.

Even hot weather plants need some period of acclimatization. Environmental changes, either slight or extreme, can throw a plant into stress. I once took a Master Gardener telephone call from a very concerned lady who told me that her potted New Guinea impatiens (*Impatiens hawkeri*) had up and died. They had performed splendidly on her patio somewhere up north, but when she brought them down to Charleston (it was August) and put them on her deck, they had slowly wilted and died. The plant label said they would grow in full sun and they had performed splendidly before coming south.

Although it can get tiresome moving potted plants around, their chances for survival greatly increase if they are gradually exposed to higher (or lower) temperatures. It doesn't matter if one is moving them from indoors to out; from the retail nursery to your home; or from one part of the country to another. The same is true for sun exposure. Most of us forget that moving even slightly south places us closer to the equator.

Many plants that enjoy the full summer sun up north will be much happier in southern climes if they are given dappled or early morning sun only. Although I have never carried a thermometer with me on a run, the physical difference between running on a shaded street as opposed to a sunny one is remarkable. Afternoon western sun usually has the intensity of a blast furnace in the southeast, so it's important to remember that plants growing near a hot city street are often subjected to even higher temperatures. The same is true for buddies kept captive in pots or flower boxes.

But let's return to our friend from the north. She wanted to know exactly why her impatiens died and suggested that it was somehow Charleston's fault. She was absolutely right. It's our location. Our weather figuratively ran her flowers to death.

To perform well, both runners and plants need carbohydrates because they are a primary source of energy. That's why competitive runners eat pasta the night before a race and fresh fruit right after a race. They are stocking up on or replenishing complex carbohydrates. Plants, on the other hand, make their own special mix of carbohydrates through photosynthesis. They require these carbs in order to make more plant parts. When plants, like runners, get low on carbohydrates, they lose big doses of energy. Runners call it "hitting the wall." Throw in the stresses of heat and humidity and an energy-depleted runner or plant faces even more dangerous consequences.

Plants are amazingly self-contained. Forever stuck in one place (until we transplant them), their systems chug along, producing food, regulating internal temperatures, and making cells for stems, leaves, roots, flowers, and seeds. All they require is a little water and some sunlight. But expose many of them to too much heat and humidity and their systems can begin to wobble.

When a plant begins to falter from too much heat and humidity, its cells begin to weaken. As a defense, its respiration rate increases to speed up new cell production. But now the plant needs more carbohydrates in order to produce the energy required for additional respiration. This in turn means that photosynthesis will have to work overtime to make up for the carbohydrate loss. Once the plant is forced to tap into its carbohydrate reserves, it will only get weaker and weaker. Eventually, the plant, like a carb-depleted runner, will "hit the wall."

The duration of physical stress is of critical importance for both plants and

New Guinea impatiens
Impatiens hawkeri

runners. It has been my experience that some people assume that southern runners eventually become immune to the everyday discomforts of sultry summers. After all, we regularly exert ourselves above and beyond all reasonable levels of sanity. Yet most of us wouldn't dream of entering a southeastern marathon in late July or August without an extensive amount of training. The sun, heat, and humidity would literally kill us. Ask most of us to go out for six or seven miles, but not 26.2.

The same holds true for plants. Even cities in the far north experience high heat and humidity during the summer. I know my friends up there aren't exaggerating or fibbing about their weather. But it's the persistent continuance of heat and humidity that makes the difference. We southeasterners usually put up with about three months of brain-baking, shirt-soaking weather every summer while a lot of folks up north experience about half of that.

Botanists tell us that plants are most vulnerable to heat stress during midday and early afternoon. Although the percentage of relative humidity often drops during these times, the combination of the two can be deadly, especially to plants that need watering.

Sometimes gardeners assume that if it's extremely muggy, plants probably don't need additional water. One of the easiest ways to see if a plant is properly hydrated is to invest in a moisture meter. These inexpensive devices make watering decisions a snap and can prevent a gardener from over or under watering.

Understanding Plant Hardiness and Heat Zone Maps

There is nothing more frustrating than preparing a herbaceous border bed, agonizing over flower selection, crawling around on your knees for hours to plant them, only to watch your new friends slowly die before the first of June. But please, if you reach that horticultural juncture where you just want to throw in the trowel, turn on the air conditioner, wait for the cooler temperatures of autumn, take a few deep breaths, and try to relax. Gardening failures are not character flaws. Help is on the way. There are two invaluable sources of gardening information that can help you make sensible plant selections. One offers you hardiness guidelines. The other tells you how many days of hot weather to expect in a particular region.

A lot of us have learned to count on the U. S. Department of Agriculture's (USDA) Plant Hardiness Zones when making plant selections. However, the USDA is talking about *cold* hardiness and this sometimes confuses novice gardeners when they're planning summertime gardens. Hardiness zones are based on winter survivability predictions and, unless you enjoy replanting your entire landscape every year, they will help you select perennials that will survive the winter.

When Deep South gardeners caught on to the usefulness of plant hardiness ratings, being the clever and creative folks that they have always been in times of adversity, they learned to tweak the USDA's numbers. Since the zones are broken into average annual *minimum* temperatures, then "hardiness" also suggests year-round durability. We thought (or hoped) that the tenderer a plant is in winter, the more heat tolerant it should be in summer. So if a particular plant was rated hardy in Zones 9 and 10, then gardeners farther north in Zone 8 should be guaranteed that a plant can make it through their version of summertime heat. Right? Well, sometimes. Then the first threat of a big chill sends us scrambling to keep these not-so-cold-hardy plants alive during the winter. There's nothing like playing a horticultural game of chance when the cards are already stacked against us.

This is because the average annual minimum temperatures for each of the eleven USDA Hardiness Zones increase in increments of 10 degrees. That's something most of us don't consider during the exhilaration of springtime. For example, Zone 9's average annual minimum temperatures are from 20 degrees to 30 degrees and Zone 8 drops to 10 degrees to 20 degrees. Once any plant gets clobbered with a temperature below its threshold, it's gone. Just a two-degree drop in temperature can permanently knock out many subtropical plants. And most of us don't live in the subtropics, even though we assume we do.

USDA Plant Hardiness Zone Map

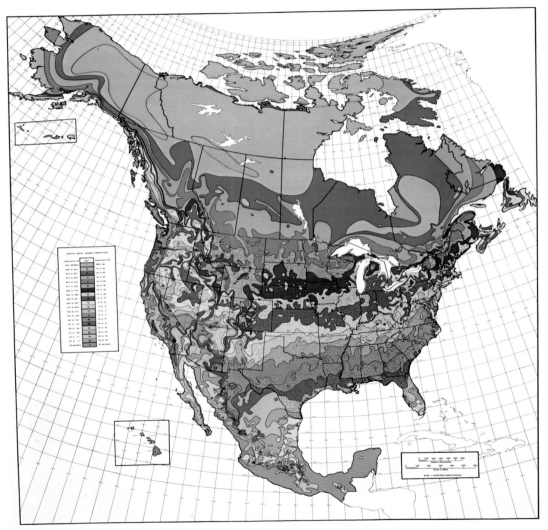

American Horticultural Society Heat Zones

It's pretty easy to know when a plant has been killed in a freeze, but heat-related deaths aren't always easy to recognize. Since many herbaceous plants express heat stress more rapidly than their woody cousins do, our annuals and perennials are often the ones we panic over first. Then we drive ourselves nuts with worry. Is it the pH? Did I add too much or not enough fertilizer? Maybe it needs water. Maybe I've overwatered. And let's not forget the all-time favorite garden ritual: spray and pray. (And if a plant doesn't look better in a couple of hours, spray it again!)

Thank goodness for American Horticultural Society President Emeritus Marc Cathey. In the late 1990s, Dr. Cathey created a Heat Zone Map that finally freed gardeners in the hot climates from second-guessing plant selection. Based on the fact that plants begin a physiological decline at temperatures over 86 degrees, his map's zones are segmented into the average number of "heat days." Zone 12, which is the hottest, has an average of 210 days above 86 degrees; while Zone 1 has less than one.

Although the Heat Zone Map uses twelve zones instead of the USDA's eleven, the concepts are quite compatible and extremely useful. Use the Heat Zone map exactly like you use the USDA Plant Hardiness Zone map. The USDA's map determines cold hardiness, while the American Horticultural Society's Heat Zone Map measures heat hardiness. When used in tandem, they become powerful tools. The following examples show how to use both of them before making plant purchases for your garden.

Bearded iris (*Iris pumila*) remains a mainstay in many gardens—north and south. It will survive winters from USDA Hardiness Zones 4–9 and take summertime heat in AHS Heat Zones 1–9. So if you live anywhere from Green Bay, Wisconsin, to Sarasota, Florida, you should be able to enjoy bearded iris every late winter, early spring or summer (depending upon where you live) and be confident that you'll see sword-shaped, dark green leaves push out of the earth the following year. On the other hand, if you live anywhere north of

American Horticultural Society Plant Heat-Zone Map

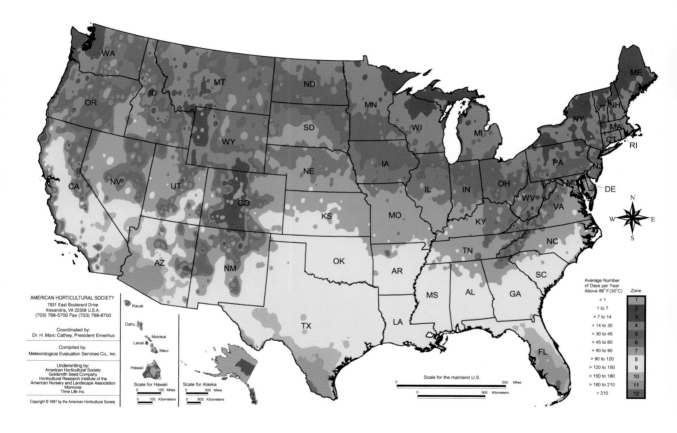

Reproduced with permission of the American Horticultural Society (www.ahs.org)

Sarasota and want to grow the spectacularly showy bird of paradise (*Strelitzia reginae*), be prepared to haul it in during the winter. Although it will do just fine in the summer from AHS Heat Zones 1–12, it is only USDA Hardy in Zones 9–11.

Note that it's never safe to assume that Hardiness Zone ratings and Heat Zone ratings will always be the same or nearly the same. It just turns out that a lot of places share the same number. Although much of the Deep South is in Hardiness Zone 8, some areas are in Heat Zone 9, and even 10. It should also be noted that many communities right along the eastern seaboard are considered to be in Heat Zone 7. It has been my observation that my daily sum-

mertime high temperatures often exceed the official recorded high from the Custom House, which is located slightly closer to the Charleston Harbor than my garden. For people right along the coast, I suggest paying close attention to your outdoor thermometers and err on the side of Heat Zone 8 to be on the safe side.

I mentioned earlier that a lot of plants begin to falter at 86 degrees. At that temperature, their cells begin to collapse. It turns out that 86 percent relative humidity is also an unlucky number for many plants. Numerous diseases begin to thrive at that moisture level, so it's important to select plants that will not succumb to the "86/86" malady. The following table shows just how vulnerable Deep South gardens are to the perils of heat and humidity.

Average Relative Humidities

Average Number of Heat Days (based on AHS Heat Zone ratings)

City	Annual Average Relative Humidity Morning/Evening	July and August Average Relative Humidity Morning/Evening	Average Number of Heat Days above 86°
Birmingham, AL	84/60%	July: 86/61 Aug: 87/60	90-120
Mobile, AL	87/62%	July: 90/65 Aug: 91/65	90-120
Montgomery, AL	86/60%	July: 90/63 Aug: 91/63	90-150
Little Rock, AR	83/59%	July: 86/58 Aug: 85/57	90-120
Jacksonville, FL	89/56%	July: 89/59 Aug: 91/61	120-150
Tallahassee, FL	90/55%	July: 94/61 Aug: 95/61	120-150
Atlanta, GA	82/56%	July: 88/59 Aug: 89/60	60–90
Savannah, GA	86/54%	July: 89/57 Aug: 91/60	90–120
Baton Rouge, LA	89/63%	July: 92/66 Aug: 92/65	120–150
New Orleans, LA	87/65%	July: 91/68 Aug: 91/68	120–150
Jackson, MS	90/61%	July: 93/63 Aug: 94/62	120–150
Asheville, NC	90/57%	July: 95/62 Aug: 97/63	30–45
Raleigh, NC	85/54%	July: 89/58 Aug: 92/59	60–90
Charleston, SC	86/56%	July: 88/62 Aug: 90/63	60–90
Chattanooga, TN	86/56%	July: 89/57 Aug: 91/57	60–90
Galveston, TX	83/72%	July: 81/70 Aug: 81/69	60–90
Houston, TX	90/64%	July: 92/62 Aug: 92/62	120–150
Norfolk, VA	78/52%	July: 81/59 Aug: 84/62	45–90
Richmond, VA	83/53%	July: 85/56 Aug: 89/57	60–90

Frost and Freeze Predictions

At first blush, it might seem silly to discuss frosts and freezes in a book about gardening in hot and humid weather. But we need to know when to set out our plants or sow seed in the spring. Too often we are unsure when to do this, but how can we begin acclimatizing our summertime seedlings if we don't know when it's safe to put them out? Seed packets often recommend sowing after the last threat of frost, but those small packets only have room for generalized information. Where do we find more specific advice?

I assume that almost every county extension service has something like "Average Frost and Freeze Dates" readily available. However, since I long ago tired of the "Call your local extension office for this information" statement, I have compiled a list of major southern cities' annual frost and freeze dates. Yes, the dates are still more generalized than some of us would like, but they should help you narrow down your window of opportunity for spring planting. If you're still anxious about when to plant or sow seed, perhaps that call to your nearest county agent is in order.

Before you use this chart, it's important to understand that these predicted dates are based on statistical probabilities. The National Oceanic and Atmospheric Administration's (NOAA) National Climatic Data Center (NCDC) keeps temperature records from hundreds of places around the United States. Using these compilations they can predict that on a certain date, the Probability Level (PrbLvl) of a freeze is at a certain percent. (This is analogous to the weatherman calling for a 20 percent chance of rain.)

Please note that some of the cities that are listed on "Average Relative Humidities Average Number of Heat Days" chart are not included below. This is because NOAA's recording devices are not located in Montgomery, Little Rock, Jacksonville, Atlanta, Baton Rouge, Jackson, or Houston. However, I have selected other areas in the regions to make up for the missing information. NOAA's complete data base can be found at http://www.ncdc.noaa.gov/oa/documentlibrary/freezefrost/freezefrost.pdf.

Ending and Beginning Frost and Freeze Dates

City	State	Spring 90%PrbLvl	Spring 50%PrbLvl	Spring 10%PrbLvl	Fall 10%PrbLvl	Fall 50%PrbLvl	Fall 90%PrbLvl
Birmingham	AL	13-Mar	29-Mar	14-Apr	24-Oct	6-Nov	18-Nov
Clanton	AL	17-Mar	30-Mar	11-Apr	18-Oct	30-Oct	11-Nov
Mobile	AL	6-Feb	27-Feb	19-Mar	5-Nov	26-Nov	17-Dec
Selma	AL	22-Feb	11-Mar	28-Mar	29-Oct	12-Nov	25-Nov
Union Springs	AL	2-Mar	18-Mar	3-Apr	22-Oct	9-Nov	22-Nov
Benton	AR	28-Mar	7-Apr	17-Apr	12-Oct	25-Oct	7-Nov
Conway	AR	21-Mar	3-Apr	16-Apr	18-Oct	31-Oct	12-Nov
Stuttgart	AR	6-Mar	23-Mar	9-Apr	23-Oct	5-Nov	18-Nov
Jacksonville Beach	FL	17-Jan	14-Feb	14-Mar	16-Nov	14-Dec	13-Jan
Lake City	FL	21-Feb	10-Mar	27-Mar	5-Nov	22-Nov	8-Dec
Tallahassee	FL	17-Feb	12-Mar	5-Apr	28-Oct	14-Nov	2-Dec
Athens	GA	16-Mar	28-Mar	10-Apr	25-Oct	8-Nov	22-Nov
Carrollton	GA	25-Mar	6-Apr	17-Apr	12-Oct	28-Oct	12-Nov
Gainesville	GA	19-Mar	3-Apr	18-Apr	23-Oct	6-Nov	20-Nov
Macon	GA	27-Feb	17-Mar	4-Apr	25-Oct	8-Nov	22-Nov
Savannah	GA	17-Feb	10-Mar	30-Mar	31-Oct	15-Nov	1-Dec
Amite	LA	24-Feb	10-Mar	25-Mar	28-Oct	14-Nov	30-Nov
Covington	LA	26-Feb	14-Mar	29-Mar	27-Oct	11-Nov	26-Nov
Lafayette	LA	23-Jan	18-Feb	17-Mar	6-Nov	26-Nov	17-Dec
New Orleans	LA	21-Jan	20-Feb	21-Mar	15-Nov	5-Dec	25-Dec
Batesville	MS	24-Mar	4-Apr	14-Apr	14-Oct	27-Oct	8-Nov
Hattiesburg	MS	1-Mar	17-Mar	3-Apr	24-Oct	8-Nov	23-Nov
Vicksburg	MS	18-Feb	13-Mar	4-Apr	29-Oct	18-Nov	8-Dec
Asheville	NC	28-Mar	10-Apr	24-Apr	11-Oct	24-Oct	6-Nov
Raleigh	NC	18-Mar	31-Mar	13-Apr	19-Oct	5-Nov	22-Nov

Ending and Beginning Frost and Freeze Dates (continued)

City	State	Spring 90%PrbLvl	Spring 50%PrbLvl	Spring 10%PrbLvl	Fall 10%PrbLvl	Fall 50%PrbLvl	Fall 90%PrbLvl
Charleston (AP)	SC	27-Feb	18-Mar	6-Apr	30-Oct	12-Nov	26-Nov
Charleston (City)	SC	23-Jan	17-Feb	14-Mar	20-Nov	10-Dec	30-Dec
Chattanooga	TN	23-Mar	05-Apr	18-Apr	19-Oct	1-Nov	14-Nov
College Station	TX	14-Feb	7-Mar	27-Mar	5-Nov	28-Nov	21-Dec
Conroe	TX	14-Feb	5-Mar	24-Mar	6-Nov	25-Nov	14-Dec
Galveston	TX	-	28-Jan	25-Feb	10-Dec	9-Jan	-
Liberty	TX	8-Feb	3-Mar	25-Mar	2-Nov	17-Nov	2-Dec
Norfolk	VA	8-Mar	23-Mar	6-Apr	31-Oct	17-Nov	4-Dec
Richmond	VA	25-Mar	10-Apr	27-Apr	13-Oct	26-Oct	7-Nov

Getting Started

Creating a new herbaceous border or revitalizing an existing one can be exhilarating. It can also be downright frightening if you're adrift in an unfamiliar sea of horticultural requirements.

Think of this chapter as a navigational chart. And if you get lost now and then, don't panic. Figuring things out can be half the fun of gardening, so just relax and enjoy the trip.

Keep in mind that, if you are unaccustomed to growing plants in a particular USDA Hardiness Zone, modifying those old, carefully thought out gardening practices can be unnerving. What used to work in cooler, dryer climates often fizzles in hot and humid ones. (I once saw someone burst into tears because spinach won't grow in Charleston's June heat.) Please don't throw in the trowel over a few disappointments. I promise that a green thumb will eventually replace the brown one.

Soils

It has been my observation as a Master Gardener that, when it comes to herbaceous plants, folks often work themselves into high snits about soil and water. Relax and think vegetables. If you can grow a tomato in a pot or a cucumber along a fence, then annuals and perennials should be a snap. Most of these plants, edibles and not, require a pH between 6 and 8; soil that is rich in organic material; and about one inch of water per week. (This translates into about 75 gallons for a 100-square-foot plot.) To some, this straightforward criteria may sound just too easy.

Yes, it's true that the hot and humid Southeast has soil that leans toward the acidic side. However, long ago, annuals and perennials had to adapt to inconsistent pH levels in order to survive in the wild. Their domesticated great-great-grandchildren now live in our gardens and still carry that genetic code.

A pH of 6 is slightly acidic while 8 is designated as a weak base. Seven, being neutral, is right in the middle of the pH scale that runs from 1–14. It is impossible to nail down the exact pH in one's soil, and more importantly how to adjust it, without having the soil professionally tested. Gardeners who suspect that their pH is off and try to fix it themselves are playing chemical roulette. Tossing a handful of dolomitic lime on a sick plant serves no purpose.

Besides, it takes about three months for the lime to affect the pH. By that time your poor patient (or is it victim?) will have probably been sent to the compost pile.

At least in the end it will have helped other plants in the garden by becoming organic material, which is probably the biggest thing missing from southeastern garden soils. We can't get enough of this stuff and we desperately need it. Our temperate climate, the very thing that brought so many of us to the South, is like a giant compost bin gone berserk. Decaying plant and animal matter, the stuff that organic material is made of, breaks down very quickly in our hot and humid environment. As a result, we must replenish our garden beds with compost or other similar products frequently.

But why do we need so much compost? Blame it on ancient oceans and Precambrian mountains. Along much of the coastal plain the soil is usually defined as sandy loam, even though we all know there is certainly more sand than loam in our gardens. Gardeners further inland are literally stuck with an opposite problem—an abundance of gooey, often red, clay. Logic tells us that if we could mix those two soil types together, we'd end up with the perfect combination for our flowerbeds. Unfortunately, that's not the case. Adding one extreme to the other may help slightly, but it's more of a psychological boost to gardeners because they want this idea to work and at least they've tried to solve the problem. Instead of shoveling or rearranging copious amounts of sand or clay, it makes more sense to simply amend both soil types with lots of organic material such as compost or dehydrated manures.

In sandy soils, compost works like a sponge to hold water. When mixed with clay soils, it loosens the goo, which makes it more friable or crumbly. The goal of the gardener is to create a soil environment where enough water is retained for plant growth and the rest drains away easily. This combination also allows oxygen to move through the soil freely and mineral particles to stay suspended in small clusters. Compost also contains carbon, which keeps beneficial bacteria alive.

Of course, organic matter also serves as a food source for plants. However, a solitary diet of this stuff does not guarantee well-fed plants. On average, most organic material contains less than 5 percent nitrogen and, of course, it doesn't stick around long in the soil. This is why commercial fertilizers shouldn't be ignored, especially for heavy feeders such as impatiens (*Impatiens wallerana*).

If there is a downside to using any kind of organic material, it's that it must be regularly replenished. It's important to remember that organic material will eventually break down and disappear. The good news is that simply side-dressing a bed with additional compost or manure after a heavy bout of rain may be all that is needed. Sometimes writing down when and why the soil was amended can help to prevent disappointment later in the season.

Light

Gardeners seem to have very personal interpretations about light requirements. To some, if the sun is shining on a particular plant when they walk out the door in the morning, then that plant is receiving full sun. To others, if a section of the garden is obscured from the sun when they return home in the evening, then that, by golly, is shade.

One of the challenges to gardening in Dixie is finding landscape locations that will offer plants enough sunlight without cooking the life out of them. Plants that can take sun and shade are always better off if they can avoid big doses of hot afternoon direct sun.

Our plants would be much happier if we could come to an agreement about how much sun is enough or too much. If plants could read, they might cheer about the following guidelines:

Full Sun: 6–8 hours of direct sunlight per day.

Filtered Sun: Sunlight that shines through trees, large shrubs, or a structure such as a pergola.

Partial Shade: 3–5 hours of direct sunlight per day.

Light Shade: 2–3 hours of shade per day.

Shade: Less than 2 hours of direct sunlight per day.

Keeping a Gardening Log

I started a gardening log simply because I was trying to identify a plant and I needed a place to jot down notes. That was almost twenty years ago. My tattered, well-used Indiana University notebook now bulges with esoteric gardening facts, book references, and planting dates. I'm probably the only person who would find this journal useful. But it doesn't matter and that's just the point. It's *my* journal for *my* garden. Everyone should keep one because it's hard to figure out where you're going if you ignore where you've just been. It doesn't matter what the journal looks like or how the information is set up. Shoot for something that will eventually evolve into an easy-to-use tool that is frequently consulted and occasionally updated.

In addition to keeping a gardening journal, I also save empty seed packets and plant tags. Why bother to copy all that information over in a log? Jot down the date sown or planted on the packet or plant tag and keep all of this together. I'm still kicking myself for not saving a packet of geranium seeds. I grew one plant that lasted almost three years before it finally succumbed to stem rot. Unfortunately, I don't remember the name of the cultivar so I'll never have an opportunity to grow another one.

It shouldn't surprise anyone that there are more entries in my journal about annuals and perennials than woody ornamentals. That's because they often demand more care and attention. They also don't stay around the garden as long as woodies. After all, who ever heard of a sixty-year-old hibiscus or verbena? But shorter lives mean more opportunities for experimentation. If some-

thing doesn't live up to your expectations, make a note of it and plant something different the next time.

Think of annuals and perennials as foils and accents to your garden's overall effect. Once you have established your landscape's foundation with trees, shrubs, and ornamental grasses, then it is time to accessorize.

We've all been in those horticultural "it needs something" situations. Even a modest herbaceous border or a few annuals growing in pots can pull a garden together. Another special thing about annuals and perennials is that just a few of them can make an unfamiliar place seem like home.

It's All About Sex

Several years ago in early spring, while I was answering gardening questions at the extension's Master Gardener office, a minister called to ask about roses. "What do they do when they're not blooming?" he asked. It was a late Thursday afternoon and he needed this question answered before he could finish his sermon for Sunday. "They're resting," I said. "They're gathering energy so they can bloom again."

"But why do they bloom in the first place?"

"So they can reproduce. The sole purpose of any plant is to make more plants."

I remember that conversation with amusement because what I was gently suggesting to this man of the cloth is that sex is everywhere in the garden. It's too bad that we don't pay more attention to this non-stop orgy. If we did, our annuals and perennials would have much more abundant bloom.

It might come as a shock to some that our prized flowers are nothing more than sexual organs surrounded by come-hither petals. Razzle-dazzle bloom was never intended for our pleasure. Instead, those fragrant, showy, vibrantly colorful flowers that we toil and worry over only exist to attract pollinators. Without these intermediaries, there would be very few plants. This is a story about sex.

Located near a flower's corolla are male stamens. This is where pollen is produced and then released through the anther. If the innermost part of the blossom is also equipped with a female carpel, which houses the ovary and ovule, the whole package is botanically defined as a "perfect flower." Not all blossoms are built from the same blueprint. Some have male and female flowers on the same plant. Others are single-sexed. Regardless of the flower's sexual arrangement, the object is always to get the pollen down into the ovary. When things go right, the ovules eventually turn into seeds. The trick is coming up with a way to make the sexual connection.

Although some plants are wind pollinated, many must rely on insects to get the pollen at least to the top of the carpel's stigma. It appears then that the first thing a plant needs is good advertising, but that doesn't turn out to be the case. Wind-pollen ancestors survived by producing sticky substances that caught the males' contributions. Beetles discovered this culinary treat and became repeat customers. More visits meant more seeds. As the plant population grew larger, competition forced some to offer better products. Sweet-tasting nectar became quite popular. Business became more cutthroat so plants began announcing their gourmet meals with colorful flowers. However, this advertising scheme worked too well. Now there were too many promiscuous pollinators. Valuable pollen was wasted when deposited on other species that couldn't use it.

Getting more pollen to moms produces more babies and perpetuates the species. In order to keep precious pollen from being delivered to just anyone, some plants began accommodating specialized intermediaries such as butterflies with long proboscises. In turn, bees and other insects became selective about whom they visited. They had become hooked on brand names and designer labels instead of mass-marketed products.

Gardeners can use a plant's sex drive to their advantage once they understand the rules of the orgy. If we want our flowers to keep blooming, we must stop the plants from hitting their reproductive stride. The extra energy they've stored for seed production must be diverted back to more flower production. We can do that by deadheading spent flower blossoms. Not only does this improve the appearance of our plants, but it also forces them to make more flowers.

Although the word "deadheading" is a silly gardening term, some take its meaning literally and wait until the flowers have dried up before pinching off the spent blooms. Even before the ovule begins to swell with seeds, the plant "thinks" it has completed its goal of procreation and will therefore stop flowering. Nervous Nellies who are reluctant to remove a single blossom before the first hint of petal fade should relax. Continuous pinching, including a few unintended snips now and then, will not only keep the plants in bloom but will improve their overall appearance. Even keeping a plant from blooming for an extended period has its rewards.

A city horticulture department was once asked to provide hundreds of potted blooming garden mums for an important function. The problem was that there was no extra money in the budget for such an extravagance. Instead, the staff started hundreds of yellow marigolds (*Tagetes* spp.) and refused to let them bloom for most of the summer. Shortly before the event, they stopped pinching the marigolds back. Their budget-on-a-shoestring plants exploded with spectacular bloom.

Sometimes gardeners are apprehensive about their deadheading techniques. The general rule is to pinch, snip, or cut back the flower stem to the

Wax begonia
Begonia semperflorens

joint above the first pair of leaves. However it is performed— with a thumbnail and index finger, a small sharp knife, scissors or pruners—the cut should be clean. Ripped and jagged stems are more prone to disease. If the overall foliage also needs sprucing, one-third of it may be removed at a time.

I have seen some people pluck off only the flower petals and think they are deadheading. However, all they have done is denude the flower, leaving the seed to continue maturing.

Annuals, because they are short-lived and do not have the leisure of taking their time to make seed, must produce it quickly. For the gardener, this means more frequent deadheading than on slower, seed-producing perennials. I have been told that some annuals such as wax begonias (*Begonia semperflorens*) and vinca (*Catharanthus roseus*) don't need to be deadheaded. I disagree. True, their spent flowers don't look as scruffy as others do, and begonia blooms do eventually fall off by themselves. However, begonias look neater if aging flowers are removed. Vincas can get leggy and yellow by mid-summer and part of that is attributable to reproduction. Look for very thin, oval clusters of vinca seedpods. This is why flowering has slowed. Cut the stems by one-third to remove most of the seed vessels. Then give the vincas a moderate dose of balanced fertilizer and they will look better in no time.

Vinca
Catharanthus roseus

Sowing Seed
In and
Out-Of-Doors

In situ means "in the place" and some annuals, plus a few perennials, prefer not to have their seed sown in manmade, climate-controlled situations. They are the ones who resent being transplanted to permanent, outdoors-garden spots. They are happiest when their seed is broadcast where it's intended to always grow.

Unfortunately, this method makes some gardeners uneasy. There are just too many uncontrollable variables that can wreak havoc on a carefully planned garden. Squirrels and domestic animals probably come to mind first, and too much or too little rain can also be a problem. There can also be a mental roadblock to planting annuals and perennials *in situ* because we usually associate this kind of gardening with vegetables. Perhaps it's time to reevaluate our necessity to always start seed in tiny little pots before planting them outside.

I too have cringed at the thought of scattering seed in a garden plot. This was after some disappointments, although most of them could have been avoided if I had only had a little more common sense and a whole lot more information. The following is what I have learned:

• I highly recommend covering *in situ* plots while applying preemergent herbicides to lawns. This also holds for areas where seed from last year's plants are expected to germinate. Preemergents work by stopping weed seeds from germinating, but they cannot always discriminate between our notion of desirable and undesirable. It doesn't matter if you scatter seed before or after the preemergent goes down. The important thing is to keep every speck of it out of your garden plot.

• If the seed packet says to sow after the last frost date, then get this task done as soon as possible. *In situ* seeds need to germinate as early as possible so the young plants are given enough time to acclimatize themselves to our harsh southern summers. If your garden is an old friend and you feel comfortable with how it usually reacts to winter's caprices, you might be able to push up the time and sow a few weeks earlier than the general last frost date prediction. However, it might be prudent to have extra seed on hand in case Mother Nature reminds you who's really in charge.

• One of the truly vexing problems with *in situ* sowing is identifying the desirable plants when they emerge from the soil. Are those newly sprouted dicotyledons just weeds or much-anticipated new friends? Many gardeners depend on *Parks Success with Seed* for foolproof seedling identification. The close-up photographs of very young plants are sharp and large enough to take the guesswork out of recognition.

Balsam
Impatiens balsamina

• Some seeds, such as *Impatiens balsamina*, need light to germinate. Covering the seeded area with glass or Plexiglas will protect the seeds from high winds and torrential downpours. It will also help to retain soil moisture, which is a must for humidity-loving seeds like *I. balsamina.*

• Watering newly planted seeds can be challenging. A forceful, coarse spray from a garden hose can knock them out of their proper sowing depth, but chances are you'll never know that because you can't see the seeds. A fine mist is preferable, but this chore takes much longer than most of us care to put up with. The water must penetrate below the planting depth and simply spraying the surface until it glistens is often not enough. A watering can with a rosette can be an invaluable tool for this task and a moisture meter will aid in assuring that enough water has been used.

• If you are concerned about intruders scratching, digging, or walking through your carefully seeded bed, cover it with 1/2-inch hardware cloth. The green-colored kind is unnoticeable and even blends in with mulch. Four-legged animals don't like to walk on it (it does them no harm), it thwarts digging, and if you forget and walk on the bed, the weave helps to distribute your footsteps.

• I offer one final suggestion about *in situ* sowing. The soil must be as carefully prepared as in a vegetable garden. A thoroughly tilled plot that's been amended with any organic material of your choice will greatly increase your chances for success. I suspect this is one of the reasons why so many wild flower kits fell out of favor. Many gardeners didn't bother to read the instructions on the container. Instead, they just tossed out the seeds, expecting a picture-perfect collection of colorful flowers for their meager efforts.

Vinca
Catharanthus roseus

Although there are certainly other perennials and annuals that prefer in situ sowing, the following ones are easy to grow and should add color to a summertime southern garden.

Vinca, Madagascar periwinkle
Catharanthus roseus (Formerly *Rosa vinca*)
Perennial and annual

I was about seven or eight years old when I first noticed vinca. I was so taken with it that I snapped a black-and-white photograph of it with my Kodak Brownie. I still have the camera (and the picture, I think) and I remain positively smitten with this immigrant from the island of Madagascar. Yes, it's been overused and some consider it nothing more than a "shopping center" plant. However, I hardly think it's fair to knock a plant that blooms all summer long, laughs at drought, and ignores high heat and humidity. It self-seeds profusely—almost too much. Instead of tossing out newly emerged plants, I try to find them new homes. But this usually lasts for only a couple of weeks because the seedlings keep coming and coming. Many of them end up in the compost because I can't keep up with the population explosion.

Vincas need full sun and well-drained soil. If you or your irrigation system sprays them regularly, they will return the favor with a healthy dose of root rot or some other type of near-fatal fungal disease.

Vincas can be heavy feeders and will benefit from a few applications of fertilizer. Look for signs of light green to yellow leaves. They are trying to tell you they're low on nitrogen. However, moderation is imperative. A sudden dose of too much nitrogen is also a surefire guarantee for disease, especially after excessive rains. These plants respond well to moderate pruning, but if you don't like deadheading or pinching, then skip this chore. Besides, most vincas never grow more than 12 inches tall. However, removing seed producing spent blossoms will encourage more flowers.

I have read that vincas prefer a slightly acidic soil (5.4–5.8), but I wouldn't worry about pH unless something looks terribly wrong, such as stunted plants and yellow leaves that don't respond to fertilizer. I have not had the soil tested in the flowerbed that holds our vinca for almost ten years. A concrete wall foundation for a wrought iron fence continuously leaches calcium carbonate into the soil, which in turn raises the pH. The vinca doesn't seem to mind.

The fun thing about vinca is that it looks good almost anywhere. Yes, even in shopping centers. It's the perfect plant for pots or flower boxes. A single plant can cheer up a rather drab spot in a garden and a massive planting along a walkway can lend interest to an otherwise boring path. It also makes a great streetscape plant. I have seen lots of it growing along curbs in downtown Charleston. The additional heat from the street doesn't phase it, even during the hottest part of the day.

Vinca prefers full sun but will grow in partial shade. Just expect fewer blooms. It is considered a perennial in USDA Hardiness Zones 9–11. However, I have seen plants with stems slightly thicker than a pencil bounce back after a mild winter in Zone 8b. But that hardly matters because the seed will give you more than you will really want the following season.

Perhaps one of the reasons why some got bored with vinca was the color selection. For years we were more or less stuck with three flower colors: pink, dark lavender and a white with either reddish-pink or yellow eyes. However, breeders can now tempt even the biggest gardening snobs with various shades of red, magenta, and pink. My favorite, 'Orchid Stardust,' is magenta with a white center and a yellow eye. 'Icy Pink Cooler' is a pale dainty pink, while 'Pacifica Red' is as bright and showy as a sports car.

USDA Hardiness Zones 9–11. AHS Heat Zones 12–1.

Coreopsis, Tickseed
Coreopsis tinctoria
Self-seeding perennial and annual

Although *Coreopsis tinctoria* is now considered native in a large part of the U.S., we gardeners were the ones who helped it along in its travels. Originally from Minnesota and west to the Canadian province of Manitoba, it escaped from flowerbeds and headed east. But this happened a very long time ago, so it's understandable why so many assume that the perky little tickseed has always been one of their states' native instead of naturalized wildflowers.

Coreopsis might not be for everyone because some might find it a little too wild looking. (After all, it *is* a wildflower.) Perhaps it looks best in cottage or informal gardens. One might also argue that we don't need another bright yellow, daisy-shaped flower with a dark red center and magenta eye. But what if I mention that it is one of the few annuals that will grow in damp or soggy sites? That information might change a few minds about this incredibly tough little plant.

Coreopsis is quite easy to grow and prefers to be grown *in situ.* Since they look best when crowded together, pluck out seedlings to only 6 inches apart. (An ounce of seed will cover about 1,300 square feet.) Deep South gardeners can plant seed in the spring or in late fall. If broadcast in the spring, the flowers will begin to appear about 70 days after sowing. Autumn sown plants may be slightly sturdier and will probably start blooming around July. No matter when they are started, tickseeds will bloom into October.

Now for some not-so-good news. Coreopsis will poop out if it is not regularly deadheaded. This chore can get old when even early evening temperatures and relative humidities get stuck at 86/86 for days on end. My only suggestion is to wait until your horticultural neatness threshold is about to snap and then grab the garden shears. Cutting back the plants, no matter if it is done recklessly, should get them blooming again.

Tickseed is quite famous for its ability to withstand drought. Its only requirement is that it receives full sun. It grows to a height of about 3 feet with a 6-inch spread, which is why it is important to grow them close together. They appreciate the support from one another.

USDA Hardiness Zones 4–9; AHS Heat Zones 12–1.

Balsam
Impatiens balsamina
Annual

It's too bad that the wildly popular *Impatiens wallerana* (I have also seen it spelled *walleriana* in seed catalogs) has upstaged its sweet cousin, *I. balsaminas*. This is unfortunate because balsams can offer a pleasant summertime diversion from those omnipresent impatiens. Balsams' camellia-like flowers are more textured and three-dimensional than flat-petaled impatiens blossoms. Yes, impatiens will always win in a color brightness contest, but the demure qualities of balsams should not be ignored. Cottage and Victorian garden aficionados should definitely experiment with balsams. These annuals still look old-fashioned because breeders haven't gone nuts trying to improve them.

Balsam
Impatiens balsamina

If you are still a little nervous about *in situ* seed sowing, then start with balsams. The seeds are a manageable size so they're easy to see while you sow them. They do need light to germinate, however, and high humidity speeds the process. Cover the seeds with some old windowpane glass and they should take off in less than a week. Just remember to remove the glass at the first flush of life.

One of the advantages to starting balsams where they will grow is that they do not have robust root systems. As a result, they usually wilt after transplanting. Although they should perk up in about 48 hours, frequent watering

might be required. Once they are established they won't be quite so demanding, but even mature balsams will not withstand drought conditions.

It's too bad that the seed companies are sometimes fitful about offering balsam seed. I received a free packet of seed in an order many years ago and instantly fell in love with these old-fashioned plants. (I think the variety was 'Carombola'.) When I tried to purchase more seed the following year, I couldn't find any. Evidently, the gardening public has finally noticed balsams because I have been able to regularly purchase balsam seed for the past several years.

If you like cottage gardening, controlled chaos, or Victorian themes, balsams are definitely for you. I once grew several of them along the edge of a narrow walkway between our kitchen garden and the cookhouse. Although they received lots of morning sun, they were shaded during the height of the afternoon heat even though the vegetables next to them were still basking in blazing sunlight. Because they shared space with tomatoes and eggplant, they were guaranteed a thorough watering nearly every day.

Balsams come in almost every color and shade except blue. Some of the blossoms are speckled, such as the red and white 'Peppermint Stick' and a few look like miniature roses or camellias. One old favorite is named 'Camellia Flower'. 'Tom Thumb' is a dwarf variety. In general, balsams are 1–2 1/2 feet tall with a 6–18-inch spread.

Gardeners who live in USDA Hardiness Zone 9b or further south will have to wait until winter to enjoy balsams. These charming plants will not survive the hot summertime temperatures along coastal Texas, Louisiana, or Florida.

USDA Hardiness Zones 0–0. AHS Heat Zones 10–1.

Sowing Seeds Indoors

There is something magic about sowing seeds and I'm always amazed and delighted every time I discover the first promise of new life. We once built a 3-foot x 3-foot, indoor, heated, seed germination box and spent countless pleasurable hours watching our plants come to life. Such an undertaking may not be for everyone, but for those who would like to try such an adventure, read Roger B. Swain's chapters titled "Sowing Seeds Indoors" and "Seedlings Under Light," from his book titled *The Practical Gardener: A Guide to Breaking New Ground.*

Of course, one doesn't always need a heated box to start seed indoors. One of the best places to try is on top of a water heater or refrigerator. Such places should offer consistent temperatures, which is important for seed germination. Do keep in mind that soil temperature, not ambient air temperature, is the key to success. A soil thermometer alleviates guesswork and worry.

Gardeners often fret about when to sow seed indoors, which, of course, is a reasonable concern. Since all of the plants in this book are intended for summertime enjoyment, indoor seed sowing should take place several weeks before the last predicted frost date.

The following list of plants from this book is meant to help gardeners devise a planting layout for a heated seed germination box *before* sowing seed. It only makes sense to plant seeds with similar soil temperature requirements in the same area, and it's also prudent to group plants that need light to germinate in one spot. The list is also intended to assist gardeners who collect seed and therefore have no printed growing information from a packet. For those who purchase seed, there are sometimes slight variations on seed culture; but always trust the instructions on the back of the packet. However, I highly recommend referring to the "Needs Light to Germinate" column before sowing. Sometimes seed companies instruct gardeners to "cover the seeds lightly." That often means that those seeds need light to germinate. Unfortunately, folks don't know this, add too much soil, and end up disappointed when nothing pops up.

There are several reliable, commercially made, seed-starting mixes on the market and I recommend using them instead grabbing the first thing from the potting shed. Seed starters are light and friable, which allows fragile seedlings to easily push out from the soil. More importantly, these mixes are sterile and, therefore, free from disease. I have had some disappointments using recycled mixes, as well as a first-class disaster with a homemade compost concoction.

The double asterisks in the *in situ* are my recommendations, but this certainly doesn't mean that one can't experiment.

Seed Requirements

Botanical Name	Common Name	Needs Light to Germinate	Number of days to Germinate	Soil Temp.	Soil Type	Sowing Depth	Comments	In Situ
Bigonia capreolata	cross vine		30-90	60-70°	Peaty	Sow on surface and lightly pat into soil		
Brugmansia	angels' trumpet	Small amount of light	50-60	70-75°	Moist and do not let dry out	Sow on surface and lightly pat into soil	If seed is dry, soak 8-24 hours before sowing	
Campsis radicans	trumpet creeper		30-90	70-75°	Well	Just cover drained	Pre-chill for weeks before sowing	
Capsicum annuum	ornamental peppers		20-30	65-80°	Average	1/4 inch		
Catharanthus roseus	vinca		15-20	55-65°	Peaty and well drained	1/4 inch		**
Chrysanthemum mortifolium	garden chrysanthemum		10-18	60-70°	Peaty	1/8 inch	Annuals can be sown *in situ*	
Coreopsis spp.	coreopsis	Light	20-25	55-70°	Well drained	Sow on surface		**
Dahlia spp.	dahlia		5-20	65-70°	Peaty. Do not allow to dry out	1/16 inch		

Seed Requirements (continued)

Botanical Name	Common Name	Needs Light to Germinate	Number of days to Germinate	Soil Temp.	Soil Type	Sowing Depth	Comments	In Situ
Datura spp.	devil's trumpet		20-45	55-65°	Peaty	Sow on surface and lightly pat into soil		
Eupatorium spp.			30-90	55°	Well drained	Just cover		
Gaillardia spp.	blanket-flower	Light	15-45	70-75°	Peaty	Sow on surface and lightly pat into soil		**
Hibiscus spp.	hibiscus		15-30	75-80°	Peaty	1/16 inch	Chip and soak before sowing	
Impatience balsamina	balsam	Light	20-30	70-75°	Moist and do not let dry out	Just cover		**
Lantana spp.	lantana		40-60	70-75°	Peaty	1/8 inch	Soak 1 day in hot water water before sowing	
Leucanthemumx superbum	Shasta daisy	Light	10-20	70°	Moist and do not let dry out	Just cover		*
Plumbago auriculata	cape plumbago		20-30	70°	Well drained	Just cover	Seed grown plants are not as robust	

Seed Requirements (continued)

Botanical Name	Common Name	Needs Light to Germinate	Number of days to Germinate	Soil Temp.	Soil Type	Sowing Depth	Comments	In Situ
Portulaca spp.	Portulaca, purslane	Light	14-21	70-85°	Well drained	Sow on surface but do cover	For *in situ* sowing, scatter seeds on soil and gently rake in	*
Verbena spp.	verbena		15-90	65°	Well drained	1/16 inch	Some seeds must be pre-chilled for 2 weeks	
Zinnia spp.	zinnia		10-25	75-80°	Peaty	1/16 inch	Sow in individual pots	*

Garden Mums
and Shasta Daisies

My curiosity about chrysanthemums
began when I was about eight years old
and at my first Big Ten football game with
my father. Many of the ladies expressed
their school loyalty by wearing huge
pom-pom corsages that had college
monograms twisted from colored pipe
cleaners and displayed in the center of
the blossom.

I thought that these creations were splendid, but I had some difficulty accepting that these plump, round flowers were chrysanthemums. They looked nothing like the ones in our flowerbed.

There are between 100 and 200 species of chrysanthemums, so it's easy for adults as well as third-graders to confuse their purposes. Florists' mums are grown specifically for corsages or potted flower arrangements. Other mums are cultivated for our gardens. And, because we are never satisfied with what we have, the Shasta daisy was invented by a man who was searching for the perfect flower.

Garden mums, Chrysanthemums

Dendranthema morifolium (*Dendranthema* x *grandiflora*)

Annual or perennial

It's unfortunate that many folks in hot and humid regions treat garden mums as annuals instead of perennials. For many gardeners, it's easier to yank them out after first frost and plant more later with whatever garden centers offer. After all, the only things these plants offer during the heat and humidity of summertime are green leaves and stems that need constant pinching. Am I the only one who still loves fretting over a flowerbed with nothing but leaves and stems; savoring the sweet anticipation of a blast of bloom at the end of a worn-out summer?

The garden mums we now cultivate are probably nineteenth-century descendants of *Chrysanthemum morifolium* x *C. indicum*. Their shapes are somewhat reminiscent of dahlias and are just as varied. The National Chrysanthemum Society (www.mums.org) recognizes thirteen flower forms, or bloom classes, of garden mums. These autumn beauties come in practically every color but blue. No matter what color or shape, all garden mums are heavy feeders and need moist, well-drained soils that are rich in organic material. They prefer a balanced, slow-release fertilizer with a moderately high nitrogen rating of 14 or 15. Give these guys plenty of room with lots of full sun.

All too often gardeners plant mature nursery stock in shady areas, feeling smug when significant bloom appears during the first season. Unfortunately, efflorescence will decline significantly in the years to come.

Garden mums are sensitive to seasonal changes and, as a consequence, have adapted their growth and bloom times to specific light and darkness lengths. This characteristic is called photoperiodism and it also affects another plant commonly associated with the seasons, poinsettias.

At the peak daylight cycle, garden mums need a maximum of 2/3 light (16 hours) and 1/3 (8 hours) dark to produce healthy leaves and stems. This is why second-year garden mums perform poorly in shade. The original grower allowed them enough sunlight to bloom the first year, but they can't gather enough energy to reproduce in the proceeding years.

In addition to the long light day requirement, garden mums will not bloom until they receive opposite amounts of light and dark: 1/3 day and 2/3 night. They are referred to as short-day plants because the length of darkness is critical. Even streetlights can affect the onset of bloom. Although they may seem like prima donna plants that must always have it both ways, healthy, field-grown mums should definitely pull their own weight for several years. These are the ones that garden centers take pride in offering. Expecting most gift shop or novelty store mums to perform in the garden usually leads to disappointment.

There is no great mystery about pinching back garden mums. The object of the exercise is to keep the plants about 6 inches tall during their "we're growing leaves and stems" period. Taking off an inch or so at least once a month will produce bushier plants with more buds. Simply follow the stem down to the next leaf node and pinch off the excess using your thumb and index finger or clean, sharp pruners. Gardeners in USDA Hardiness Zone 8b and south may stop performing this chore is August. Folks in USDA Hardiness Zone 8a and north may quit in July.

Depending on the cultivar, garden mums will reach heights of 1 1/2–3 feet. Of course, their spread also varies with each variety. It's important to read the planting instructions on the plant tag. Crowding garden mums together is a surefire recipe for disease. Luther Burbank tried to tell us that almost 100 years ago but most of us, myself included, often fail to pay attention.

Garden mums will bounce back even after extended bouts with 20-degree temperatures. Cut back plants to the ground after first frost. In the Deep South, they are one of the first plants to return in late winter. Propagate by division every two years. USDA Hardiness Zones 4–10. AHS Heat Zones 12–1.

Chrysanthemums

Many years ago, a friend offered me a bucket full of "mystery" mums. They had always been part of her garden forever but she never learned their name. They are more than likely a popular post-World War II variety called 'Yellow Galaxy'. Knowing that I was a pushover for anything that resembled a daisy, she offered to share some with me. It was in early June and the daytime temperatures had already settled into hot and hotter so I was worried that my new garden mums would balk over being transplanted. I pinched them back to a few inches in height, kept them watered, and covered them with newspaper or spent sabal palmetto fronds during hot afternoons.

Although I had been warned that these fellows would shoot up to prodigious heights in no time, I wasn't prepared for such robust plants after such a short period of acclimatization. My weekly snipping kept their overall height to under 6 inches tall. When I stopped pinching off the tops in August, it was like turning caged animals loose. They went everywhere. By the time they began blooming, many of the stalks were 3 feet tall and I was scrambling to find ways to keep them upright. I couldn't stand their flopping habit but, by then, I was simply crazy about the daisylike blooms. How can anyone resist bright yellow flowers with greenish centers? And, as they aged, the petals took on an attractive pinkish hue. I was determined to find a way to make these plants behave next season. I was about to become a chrysanthemum control freak.

A horticulturist suggested that I explore using a plant growth retardant (PGR) that would slow down the hormones responsible for making stems longer. Nurserymen regularly use them on some types of young garden mums. (They also use PGRs on poinsettias. These plants can reach 4–6 feet tall in places like old sugar plantations in the Caribbean, and keeping these holiday plants squat and bushy for mass market consumption is a must.) Perhaps I could find a product that was available to home gardeners. Well, maybe—if I cared to purchase large quantities at an even larger price.

Since then, I have made these magnificent plants stand at attention with wire fences, hardware cloth cages, plastic soda six-pack rings, and black cord. However, I'm no longer as obsessive about keeping them upright. Many of them lean on one another, or the fence, and the lemon grass (*Cymbopogon citratus*) doesn't mind a little early autumn cuddling. The incorrigible stems get cut and brought inside for flower arrangements. The flowers will last up to two weeks in a vase if the water is changed every other day.

Shasta Daisy
Leucanthemum x *superbum*
Annual and perennial

The botanical name for Shasta daisy was once *Chrysanthemum* x *superbum* but now the accepted nomenclature is *Leucanthemum* x *superbum*. This assignment makes more sense because two of Miss Shasta's parents are *Leucanthemum vulgare* and the ox-eye daisy (*C. leucanthemum*). Those who are familiar with the history of this carefully bred hybrid know that this plant had at least three

Shasta Daisy
Leucanthemum x *superbum*

parents instead of the customary two. The creation of the Shasta daisy is not a simple story about a plant breeder's search for a new and improved variety. Instead, it is an epic tale about Luther Burbank's determination to build a better daisy.

Mr. Burbank (1849–1926) got it into his head that the world needed a bigger, whiter, and stronger daisy that would stand up to nearly every kind of gardening situation imaginable. He wanted folks in Alaska to enjoy his new hybrid as much as the citizens of Florida. Burbank, a Massachusetts lad, and a cousin to seed king W. Atlee Burpee, decided that daisies had the genetic spunk to flower anywhere. He had always marveled at how nonchalantly they could change and adjust themselves to different environmental conditions.

The daisy became scattered to widely separated parts of the earth with widely different climates, and it gradually became several varieties of daisy, with a common heredity, but each with its own peculiar characteristic that it had acquired through the power it had to vary and adapt itself.
(Luther Burbank with Wilbur Hall, *The Harvest of the Years,* 259)

He went on to say that three particular varieties had individual horticultural strengths. If he could genetically blend them together to get radiant white petals, strong stems to support a much taller plant, and abundant bloom, he could offer the world one heck of a daisy.

According to Hugo De Vries, Professor of Botany at the University of Amsterdam, and a contemporary of Burbank's, the first daisy for consideration was the Japanese cultivar *Nipponanthemum nipponicum*. It had already made itself at home on Burbank's farm in Santa Rosa, California. It was brilliantly white—much whiter than other field daisies—and Burbank also admired its waxy petals. He crossed this plant with the ox-eye daisy because *C. leucanthemum* had large flowers and strong, stiff stems. Although not native to America (it's sometimes called an English daisy), this plant was a champion at adapting itself to new environments. Mr. Burbank then added *Leucanthemum vulgare* to his mix. Recalling that this dingy white, yet robust, little wild daisy had been a profuse bloomer in the fields of New England, this variety might give him increased flowering.

Of course, none of this experimentation took place over a few seasons. After sorting and eliminating hundreds of thousands of plants, Burbank finally got the daisy of his dreams seventeen years later. He named it Shasta daisy after Mt. Shasta, a volcanic peak in California's Cascade Mountains.

It's too bad that we couldn't leave Mr. Burbank's creation alone because some later "new and improved" varieties are nothing more than persnickety prima donnas. The original Shasta daisy looked more like a shrub than an herbaceous perennial. There is a black-and-white photograph in his autobiography of a toddler touching a Shasta's lower flowers. They are almost as tall as the child's shoulders. Judging from this picture, the plant must have been at least 4 feet tall and just as wide. Today, the average height

Shasta Daisy
Leucanthemum x *superbum*

and width of *L.* x *superbum* varieties are about half of that.

In general, Shastas are USDA Hardy in Zones 4–9. Although they will grow in AHS Heat Zones 12–1, central and southern Floridians must treat them as winter annuals because Shastas will collapse under intense heat. They are deciduous, herbaceous perennials that favor full sun but will tolerate light shade. They have moderate drought resistance once they become established. And now for the caveats.

I have come to the conclusion that these fabulous specimens with shiny, deep green, coarsely toothed leaves are one of those plants that gardeners can either grow or can't grow. There is no in between. Shastas either accept where they have been put and reward you with dazzling bloom or they will pout themselves to death, making you feel terribly guilty in the process. Although there is not a horticulture school in the Southeast that does not recommend them for southern summertime gardens (with the exception of Florida) my bet is that most Shasta problems are heat related.

Shastas must be gently introduced to a garden before daytime temperatures get stuck in the mid-eighties and the nighttime ones refuse to drop below 70 degrees. They can't withstand sudden blasts of severe heat like the kind that can show up on an April afternoon when it suddenly reaches 83 degrees for a couple of hours. Even when they appear to have recuperated, permanent damage may have already occurred. Then, later into the growing season, they begin to slowly melt away without explanation.

Although there are many hybridized versions of Mr. Burbank's famous flower, I am particularly fond of a variety called 'White Knight'. I grew some from seed several years ago and enjoyed them until I foolishly rearranged them. I had read that Shastas look fabulous when planted among daylilies. I moved the Shastas to a daylily bed in late March, believing that was enough time for them to acclimatize. After all, they were only going from one side of a very narrow yard to the other. I should have left them where they were, under a sabal palmetto and along the wall that supports the wrought-iron fence. Both

Shasta Daisy

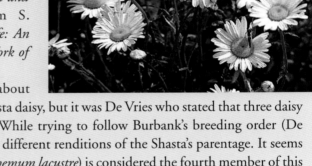

I became enthralled with the history of the Shasta daisy when I had the pleasure of surveying the Charleston Library Society's entire gardening book collection. On a dusty shelf upstairs sat two long-forgotten books. One of them was Hugo De Vries' *Plant-Breeding: Comments on the Experiments of Nilsson and Burbank.* The other was William S. Harwood's *New Creations in Plant Life: An Authoritative Account of the Life and Work of Luther Burbank.*

Both authors wrote extensively about Burbank's laborious breeding of the Shasta daisy, but it was De Vries who stated that three daisy varieties were used in the experiment. While trying to follow Burbank's breeding order (De Vries rambles), I stumbled upon several different renditions of the Shasta's parentage. It seems that the Portuguese field daisy (*Leucanthemum lacustre*) is considered the fourth member of this genetic brew. Now I was even more curious.

Knowing that Luther Burbank had written an autobiography, I hiked back over to the library. In his book, *The Harvest of the Years*, Burbank says he used three different daisies to eventually get his Shasta. I have no idea why he did not mention *L. lacustre*. However, Allan Armitage and other highly respected horticulturists tell us that four varieties eventually made up the Shasta daisy: *Chrysanthemum leucanthemum*, *Nipponanthemum nipponicum*, *Leucanthemum vulgare*, and *L. lacustre*.

For the average gardener, none of this probably matters. Burbank's determination is still a great story and the Shasta daisy is certainly an all-American plant no matter how many parents it has.

sheltered the Shastas from the hot afternoon sun. They were also growing above a soaker hose, so their leaves seldom got wet.

This relocation was a disaster. It was too hot for the Shastas, and the daylilies turned into real-estate-grabbing bullies. In addition, the daisies were now getting watered from above and the leaves started showing signs of leaf spot. The Shastas gave up their bloom much too early in the season and the ones who survived my cruelty limped into autumn.

They showed promise the following spring but then came the final blow. Just as they were beginning to bloom at the end of May, a stealth flower pick-er walked off with every blossom. Whoever thought our garden was the U-Pick kind didn't bother to bring pruners or shears, so the stems were yanked and ripped from the plants. This time our 'White Knights' never recovered. Although Shasta daisies are not long-lived perennials in southern gardens (their average life expectancy is between 2–3 years), my plants would have probably seen another season if they hadn't been so mistreated.

I didn't bother to start more seed the following year, but it wasn't because the intruder had discouraged me. I simply couldn't find a seed source. I sus-pect that 'White Knight' had been upstaged by several new introductions, espe-cially 'Becky'. She's been heavily promoted and quite popular for some time.

It's nice to see that, for the past two seasons, 'White Knight' has reappeared in the seed catalogs. Like all Shastas started from seed, they need light in order to germinate. The secret to success is carefully controlled soil moisture. Too much dampness will spoil the seed, but if allowed to dry out, the seed will not germinate. When purchasing plants, they should be planted as soon after the last frost date as possible. This will give them time to adjust to a new situation.

The following cultivars should give most southern gardeners pleasure dur-ing several hot and humid summers. Most Shastas bloom from July through August. If bloom times are different, they are listed in the "Comments" col-umn. All are for AHS Heat Zones 9–1.

Chrysanthemum
leucanthemum

Shasta Daisy Cultivars

Cultivar	Flower size	Height and Spread	USDA Hardiness Zone	Comments
'Alaska'	3" blossoms	1–3" tall 1–2' wide	USDA 3–9	An old, reliable favorite. Seeds or division.
'Becky'	3–4" blossoms	3–4' tall 40" wide	USDA 4–9	Perhaps the most robust Shasta of them all. Division.
'Crazy daisy'	3" blossoms	2–4' tall 1-1/2–2' wide	USDA 5–8	Shaggy, fluffy petals. Seeds or division.
'Silver princess'	3" blossoms	12–15" tall 1–1 1/2' wide	USDA 4–9	A dwarf variety. Blooms June-August. Seeds or division.
'Snow lady'	2 1/2" blossoms	12–36" tall	USDA 5–9	All American Selection winner.
'White knight'	5" blossoms	1 1/2–2' tall 1–1 1/2' wide	USDA 5–9	Blooms late May to first frost.

Ox-Eye Daisy

Those springtime masses of bobbing daisies seen in meadows and along roadways are probably ox-eye daisies (*Chrysanthemum leucanthemum*). These perennials can get up to 3 feet tall, but they sometimes grow to only 1–2 feet in height. They usually bear single 2-inch flowers on their stalks, but some will send out a few more. Depending on the geographical location, ox-eye daisies bloom from June to August.

This European plant was probably brought to America during the early twentieth century as an ornamental. After escaping from cultivation, it found a comfortable home in meadows and fields. Naturalized throughout most of the U.S., it is now listed in most wildflower field guides. In some regions it has become an invasive pest, so that some states have declared it a noxious weed. Farmers dislike it as much as the morning glory (*Ipomoea tricolor*) because, when dairy cattle consume it, their milk takes on an unpleasant taste. The North Carolina Botanical Garden at Chapel Hill has put *Chrysanthemum leucanthemum*, as well as *Leucanthemum vulgare*, on their "Plants to Avoid in the Southeastern United States" list.

Perennial Vines and Roses

Charleston is a city of vines and climbing roses. They are as much a part of our cultural identity as shrimp and grits and pluff mud. We use them to decorate fences and walls and to soften sharp architectural details.

Bignonia capreolata	**cross vine**
Campsis radicans	**trumpet creeper**
Clematis terniflora	**sweet autumn clematis**
Clematis virginiana	**virgin's bower**
Ficus pumila	**creeping fig**
Macfadyena unguis-cati	**cat's claw vine**
Rosa banksiae	**Lady Banks rose**
Rosa laevigata	**Cherokee rose**
Rosa x noisettiana	**Noisette rose 'Blush'**

We cultivate them to protect our privacy and to hide unattractive views or objects. We allow them sprawl up and into trees and we also plant them to attract butterflies and hummingbirds.

Many of our vines are native ones, but some come from Asia and the Caribbean. Although our cherished climber, the Noisette rose, was not "invented" in this country, one of its parents was a Charlestonian.

No matter where we live—in the city, suburbia, or the country—vines give our landscapes depth, height, and texture. Some of them, like the abundantly thorny Cherokee rose (*Rosa laevigata*), can even offer security from intruders.

Cross vine
Bignonia capreolata

All of the vines listed below are perennials. Although annual vines are fun to grow (consider them entertaining summertime experiments), in the long run, perennials are easier to care for. These often-evergreen buddies don't have to be yanked down and hauled away after the first frost and they don't need to be replanted every year.

Cross vine

Bignonia capreolata

Native perennial

The cross vine (*Bignonia capreolata*) is a southeastern native that grows in forests and clearings from Maryland down to Florida and west to Missouri and Texas. This fast growing vine has no specific horticultural requirements as long as it receives average moisture. It attaches itself to objects by tendrils, which makes it an ideal plant for hiding chainlink fences. It is sometimes described as a high-climber because it can grow up to 40 feet in length and, when given the opportunity, cross vine will gladly scramble up a tree to get more sun.

Cross vines are so named because cut stems display a cross-shaped design. The flaring tubular flowers on the wild species are reddish orange on the outside and yellow on the inside. They are about 2 inches long and dangle in clusters of three or more. The 3–5-inch, glossy green leaves turn to sort of a bronze red in winter.

There are several varieties of cross vine, but 'Tangerine Beauty' is my favorite. Like other cross vines, it offers its best bloom in spring. It has a 2–inch long tubular flower that flares into five segments. The trumpet-like bell is 1 3/4 inches wide. The outer flower tinge displays a crayon-colored texture of tangerine. The inside is yellow, while the flare is a slightly brighter orange. I have counted as many as five flowers to a cluster.

Tangerine Beauty cross vine
Bignonia capreolata
'Tangerine Beauty'

'Tangerine Beauty' cross vine's first bloom in springtime is quite robust. Although its efflorescence declines after the first explosion, it blooms off and on throughout the summer. This is good news for southeastern gardeners who plant 'Tangerine Beauty' to attract hummingbirds. In Charleston, these little buddies show up in July. Although all cross vines prefer full sun, they will sporadically bloom in part shade. Evidently, my 'Tangerine Beauty' doesn't know about this general rule. It has merrily bloomed while creeping along a section of fence that is shaded by a mature Magnolia grandiflora and a water oak. 'Tangerine Beauty' is evergreen, but has only a slight propensity to turn reddish bronze in winter. Even though it loses much of its attractiveness during the coldest months, it still makes a useful screen.

Like all cross vines, 'Tangerine Beauty' can be pruned at any time to control size. It appreciates an occasional dose of fertilizer as well as a 1–2-inch layer of mulch or fallen leaves.

Propagate by cuttings. USDA Hardiness Zones 6–9. AHS Heat Zones 1–9.

Trumpet creeper
Campsis radicans
Native perennial

As far as I am concerned, the native version of trumpet creeper (*Campsis radicans*) needs to be sent to charm school. It spreads not only from seed but also by sending out underground runners. I have found it growing in the middle of azaleas, in herbaceous borders, in lawns, and sneaking up hollies and palmettos. Never let it grow up the side of a wooden structure. It can push its way under the siding and eventually ruin it. We have purchased hundreds of ounces of nonspecific herbicide to keep it out of our landscape. I have fantasized about intravenous hookups with Roundup®.

For gardeners who are willing to put up with such bad behavior from a perennial vine, trumpet creeper prefers to be left alone. It will grow in all types of soils. Planting it by itself in an area with all-day full sun might keep its thick, woody stems away from trees, but don't count on it. This is a very sneaky vine. Of course, another way to handle it is to keep it captive in a hanging basket, allowing its flowers to spill over the sides. No matter how it is grown, the abundant, colorful, trumpetlike blossoms that appear in late summer attract hummingbirds. Even I grudgingly admit that the inflorescence of bright orange dangling over a fence can be spectacular.

To the uninformed, trumpet creeper and cross vine flowers may look alike. They are both tubular, with a five-section flare at the bell. Trumpet creeper flower color runs from yellow to red, but does not display a crayon-colored texture. While the standard wild trumpet creeper variety is orange, the following cultivars offer various hues:

Flava	**Yellow**
Speciosa	**deep orange red**
Minor	**orange and scarlet**
Crimson Trumpet	**deep red**
Atropurpurea	**Scarlet**
Praecox	**Scarlet**

Speciosa is slightly shrubbier than the standard trumpet vine that can reach 20–40 feet tall.

These deciduous plants grow on new year's growth, so whacking them back to the ground in late winter might control some of their bad behavior.

Propagate by cuttings or seeds. USDA Hardiness Zones 4–9. AHS Heat Zones 12–4 (estimated).

Sweet autumn clematis

Clematis terniflora

Perennial

Some southern gardeners quake in their Wellies when the name *Clematis terniflora* is whispered. This fabulously sweet-smelling Japanese vine has worn out its welcome in some parts. As a result, it has gained a reputation as a common criminal. It seems fitting then that this vine should have a couple of taxonomical aliases. Sweet autumn clematis is also known as *C. paniculata* or *C.*

Trumpet creeper
Campsis radicans

Sweet autumn clematis
Clematis terniflora

maximonowicziana. I mention this as a warning to gardeners who might purposely try to avoid the name *C. terniflora* and smugly return home from the garden center with *C. paniculata* or *C. maximonowicziana* believing that they have avoided purchasing the incorrigible one.

If given a little support, sweet autumn clematis's tendrils will enable it to scamper up 30-foot vertical surfaces. I witnessed one completely cover a *Camellia japonica* 'Mrs. Perkins' in about a month. Although I had an unusual looking flowering "shrub" for a few weeks, and no harm came to the camellia, untangling the vine from stems was tedious. I cut the sweet autumn clematis back to the ground and it behaved itself until the following spring. Now I see that it is about to take over poor Mrs. P. again if I don't take action soon.

Sweet autumn clematis is not choosy about soil type. Although somewhat difficult to dig up and transplant because of a stubborn root system, it will revert back to its drought-tolerant characteristics once it gets over the shock of being moved. It will need frequent watering until it is established, and cutting back some of its longer stems will reduce its need for moisture. Nursery-grown container stock is much easier to plant and recovers from transplant shock more easily.

Although some might find it absurd that gardeners actually purchase this often invasive stuff, sweet autumn clematis has two appealing attributes. It will grow in spots where other climbers absolutely refuse and its sweet-smelling, 1-inch wide, white star-shaped flowers are spectacular against the vine's dark green leaves. Even when grown in shade, the late-summer bloom is opulent. The leaves come in threes and, as a Master Gardener, I have had to assure several concerned homeowners that they are not growing poison ivy. Sweet autumn clematis's leaves are opposite while poison ivy's are alternate. Its leaves are usually evergreen in the warmer USDA Hardiness Zones 7–8 and deciduous in zones 6–5. However, I have seen vines in Charleston (8b) suffer from partial leaf dieback if temperatures drop below freezing on several consecutive nights.

Propagate by cuttings. USDA Hardiness Zones 5–8. AHS Heat Zones 12–4 (estimated).

Virgin's bower
Clematis virginiana
Native perennial

If *Clematis terniflora* is the Scarlett O'Hara of vines, then *Clematis virginiana* is Melanie Wilkes. And just like Scarlett's foil, Virgin's bower is almost too good to be true.

Virgin's bower is native to the North Carolina Appalachians. It was introduced to colonial gardens in the early 1700s and slowly made its way up the coast. Although now considered invasive in parts of the Northeast, it continues to behave itself in the south. It climbs to only 10–20 feet by using twisting and twining leaf stems called petioles. Virgin's bower will bloom in sun or partial shade from July to September.

If there is a downside to this deciduous, woody vine it is that the flowers have no scent. However, to make up for this character flaw, it produces fluffy, white, silklike strands on mature seed. The effect is rather ethereal and slightly reminiscent of cotton bolls. Virgin's bower is also not quite as hardy as sweet autumn clematis and is more particular about its habitat. It prefers a moist to wet situation, although it is not interested in soil type.

Virgin's bower
Clematis virginiana

Creeping fig
Ficus pumila

Virgin's bower flowers grow on new growth, so a vigorous spring pruning will not spoil its late summer efflorescence. It can be easily grown from seed without any special treatment such as chilling.

Propagate by cuttings. USDA Hardiness Zones 6–8. AHS Heat Zones 12–4 (estimated).

Creeping fig

Ficus pumila

Perennial

Creeping fig (*Ficus pumila*) grows so luxuriantly in Charleston that it's hard to imagine folks in northern climes pampering it as a houseplant. I recall reading a description of *F. pumila* in a book about indoor gardening that stated, on rare occasions, this variety climbs moist surfaces. Oh really? As a Deep South gardener, I can't imagine why anyone would want to grow creeping fig inside, much less in something like a shower stall. Down in Dixie we think of creeping fig as an outdoor-type pet and let it roam on vertical structures that need some interest or outright camouflaging.

Creeping fig is native to Australia, China and Japan. It might be a little difficult to believe that it is related to the rubber plant (*F. elastica*) and fig trees such as *F. benjamina,* but it is. When creeping fig is pruned, the cut stems exude a thick, white liquid that is similar to the latex found in rubber plants.

The alternate, heart-shaped leaves on creeping fig are evergreen. If they turn yellow, they are suffering from sun scorch. Creeping fig is happiest in part sun/part shade or just shade. Young leaves are usually less than 1/2-inch wide and about as long. If the plant is not periodically clipped back or is left unattended for about two years, it will take on a shaggy appearance with 3-inch-long mature leaves. Most gardeners prefer the snugged-close-to-the-wall lacy look that immature leaves lend because it offers a more formal effect. An occasional clip with hand shears or pruners whenever new growth appears is usually enough to keep creeping fig neatly coifed.

This is another vine that is nonchalant about soil types. It will put up with occasional bouts of wetness and drought. It doesn't care if it is growing in sandy soil or clay and is indifferent to pH. The only thing it can't take is salty soil.

Creeping fig may be relatively easy to take care of, but keep in mind that it does not discriminate from the kinds of vertical surfaces made available to it. If grown on a concrete wall that is adjacent to a wooden structure, it will try to cover that also. This is a vine that must be watched.

Creeping fig
Ficus pumila

Creeping fig climbs by sending out rootlike grippers that grab onto a structure. If allowed to grow on painted siding, which is certainly not recommended but happens, mature plants will leave "footprints" when yanked down. It should also be noted that once creeping fig's feet have been removed from their hold, they cannot be reattached. Prune it back to where the plant is still clinging. It grows at a moderate rate and will eventually recover the exposed area.

The general rule is that creeping fig is cold tolerant to about 20 degrees F. However, on Christmas Eve, 1989, temperatures dropped to 18 degrees F on peninsular Charleston. Practically everyone's creeping fig died back to the ground, but a lot of it slowly came back the following summer.

There are several varieties of creeping fig. 'Minima', which is often listed as *Ficus pumila minima*, has slender 1/4-inch leaves. Also called dwarf creeping fig, it is only cold tolerant to 25 degrees (USDA Hardiness Zone 9a). For gardeners who like oaklike-shaped leaves, 'Quercifolia' is a real cutie that also sports 1/4-inch leaves. But to me, the real showstopper is 'Variegata'—obviously a variegated cultivar. Its petite leaves are less than 1/2-inch long and flashed with cream-colored markings along the edges. 'Variegata' comes with only one caveat. Some variegated plants revert back to solid colors, which drives some gardeners to distraction. *Ficus pumila* 'Variegata' might lose its white markings during prolonged Deep South heat waves, but will return to its gorgeous self once cooler temperatures move in. I have heard some insist that *Ficus pumila* 'Variegata' might be cold hardy to 15 degrees and possibly a degree or two lower.

Propagate by air-layering. USDA Hardiness Zones (7)8–11. AHS Heat Zones 12–1.

Cat's Claw Vine

Macfadyena unguis-cati

Perennial

Cat's claw vine (*Macfadyena unguis-cati*) is a nonnative vine that is considered invasive in South Carolina, Georgia, Florida, Louisiana, and Texas as well as Hawaii and Puerto Rico. Although it can be a real pest, some people can't get enough of it. They fuss over it by giving it fertilizer and mulch simply because they have confused it with South Carolina's state flower, yellow or Carolina jessamine (*Gelsemium sempervirens*). Both vines bloom at about the same time

Cat's Claw Vine
Macfadyena unguis-cati

in early spring. Although Carolina jessamine's bright yellow flowers are more reminiscent of tubular trumpet creeper or cross vine blossoms, many take a quick glance at the color and then jump to the wrong conclusion. Cat's claw vine's flowers are more funnel-shaped and exhibit a vaguely orchid quality. They are about 2 1/2-inches in diameter at the five rounded flares' widest point.

Cat's claw vine is a wicked climber and can reach 40 to 50 feet tall with a spread almost as wide. In the center of its opposite, compound leaves are three clawlike tendrils. Although cat's claw vine looks fabulous when it runs along the top of brick walls or metal fences—especially when those bright yellow flowers dangle down in front of those evergreen leaves—this vine will never

Cat's Claw Vine
Macfadyena unguis-cati

stay put. It will scale anything in its way. This sneaky plant with thin, 2-inch-long leaves has the propensity to hide and blend in with surrounding trees and shrubs. Gardeners often don't realize that cat's claw vine has moved in until its brilliant flowers suddenly appear from out of nowhere. We thought we had permanently removed cat's claw vine from our 50-foot hackberry (*Celtis occidentalis*) until a spring thunderstorm blew down hundreds of yellow flowers to the ground. I still haven't figured out where it is growing from, and it may not even be on our property. Our situation is certainly not unusual in the older parts of Charleston. Because of our colonial ties to the Caribbean, my guess is that this native of the West Indies was first innocently turned loose in our ancestors' gardens as a desirable ornamental.

So am I encouraging southern gardeners to grow son-of-kudzu? No, but if someone finds cat's claw vine on their property, I wouldn't head for the Roundup®. Cat's claw is still available commercially, although Florida nurserymen are trying to discourage further production in their state.

Cat's claw vine grows in sun or shade and has no preference for soil types. It has a slight salt tolerance. This vine produces a long, slender, slightly curved, 6–7-inch pod that contains winged seeds that can be propagated.

Propagate by seeds or cuttings. USDA Hardiness Zones 8–11. AHS Heat Zones 12–1.

Roses

Rosa spp.

Up until a few years ago, I was an outright coward when it came to growing roses. All I had ever read or heard about Deep South rose care was spray, and then spray again. The pundits had managed to convince me that roses were extraordinarily delicate plants and I would therefore spend every waking hour worrying about their horticultural demands. Disease is omnipresent they said. Have you sprayed today? Why on earth should I subject myself to one more hot-weather gardening irritation?

It turns out that a fellow Master Gardener, who was determined to save me from a major gardening foible, changed my perceptions about the care and feeding of my favorite type of southern roses, the climbers. She gently demanded that I accept a Noisette 'Blush' (*Rosa* x *noisettiana*) cutting from her garden instead of turning a Cherokee rose (*Rosa laevigata*) loose in my backyard.

The Noisette was my first rose-growing experience and I have finally stopped hyperventilating every time someone suggests growing roses in the south.

Lady Banks rose
Rosa banksiae
Perennial

Many of the gardens on Charleston's peninsula are enclosed with wrought iron fences, which are perfect supports for the long, almost thornless canes of Lady Banks roses (*Rosa banksiae*). They can be easily trained to rest on the upper railing and weave in and out of the posts. These antique, evergreen-climbing roses also add continual interest to arbors, any type of fence, sheds, or garages long after they have offered up a month of efflorescence in the spring. For gardeners who don't care to have Banksia roses climbing on objects, don't despair. They also look great as pillars or just left to flop against something that offers moderate support.

Banksian roses are native from north-central through southern China. The wild version has small, white, single flowers that smell intensely of violets. A double yellow variety (*Rosa banksiae 'Lutea'*) was discovered in the Canton province and presented to England's Royal Rose Society in 1824. This is the Lady Banks rose that most

Lady Banks rose
Rosa banksiae

people associate with Deep South gardens. Two other cultivars, a double white (*Rosa banksiae 'Alba Pena'*) and a single yellow (*Rosa banksiae 'Lutescens'*) are also available.

Lady Banks 'Lutea' has soft yellow flowers with a green eye. Blossom size is quite dainty at only 3/8–5/8 inch in diameter. Although they are not scented, the bloom is always copious. This is the perfect plant to weave in and out of a fence or trellis because it will not bite the hand that cares for it; it is practically thornless. 'Lutea' is the hardiest of the Lady Banks roses although temperatures below 15 degrees will kill it. Like the rest of these roses, it is practically impervious to disease.

The double white version, 'Alba Pena', which is sometimes designated as *R. banksiae banksiae* or *R. banksiae alba*, is not quite as hardy as Lady Banks 'Lutea' and has a few more thorns. However, its 5/8–3/4-inch flowers have an intense violet fragrance.

The single cultivar, Lady Banks 'Lutescens', is not violet scented but presents its own distinctive sweet smell. Its slightly larger flowers (3/4–1 inch) will eventually set an abundance of yellow hips. Because of these slight deviations, some botanists suggest that 'Lutescens' is probably a hybrid.

For those who are interested in horticulture history, Banksia roses were named after the wife of famous plant collector and scientific adventurer Joseph Banks (1743–1820). Banks was Captain James Cook's naturalist on his famous South Seas expedition to Australia (1768–1771) and later served as director of Kew Gardens.

Lady Banks roses flower on second and third year growth and they are not repeat bloomers. They are fast climbers that will reach 15–20 feet in height. They are content to grow on beach properties because they are resistant to salt spray and salty (saline) soils. Banksia roses will tolerate poor soils as long as weeds are not allowed to intrude. Mulching helps to keep intrusive plants away and protects roots. Plant in full sun. Propagate from soft wood cuttings in the spring. USDA Hardiness Zones 7–9(10). AHS Heat Zones 9–3.

Cherokee rose
Rosa laevigata
Perennial

I had always admired two specimens of Cherokee rose growing near our property. I love the way they explode into abundant, fragrant white bloom every late March through April. Their massive canes with shiny deep green leaves block out unattractive voids that are often present in landscapes during the transition from cool to hot weather. But what really impresses me is their robust health. The behemoths that I have become so enamored of are stuck in a hot cityscape with lousy soil and plenty of air pollution. They are definitely not pampered plants yet neither ever show signs of insect nor disease damage. Wow. What a rose.

Cherokee rose
Rosa laevigata

Since our neck of downtown Charleston is billed as an eighteenth-century *suburban* neighborhood, I thought a little botanical wildness from *R. laevigata* would fit in nicely with our woodsy, edge-of-the-forest-style backyard. But more importantly, I had an unattractive fence that needed hiding and I was tired of doing battle with a neighbor's landscape crew whose wont was to rip or hack anything that grew on *my* fence. Those big, hooked, Cherokee rose thorns would certainly put a stop to their biannual ruin. However, if I had carried out this horticultural scheme, I would have undoubtedly regretted it.

Although Cherokees are botanically classified as wild roses, they are not indigenous to North America. They are native to central China, the Sichuan province, and the lower altitudes of Taiwan. No wonder they love the Deep South! *R.*

laevigata became naturalized in the southeast sometime during the seventeenth century. In fact, by the time André Michaux got around to writing about this species in 1803, he thought they were native to North America. Naturalized Cherokee roses now run wild in North and South Carolina, Georgia, Florida, Alabama, Mississippi, Louisiana, Texas, and also Hawaii. While it's the much-loved state flower of Georgia, Floridians include it in their official invasive nonnative plant list. It has also outworn its welcome in parts of Texas and Alabama. No matter where you live, it can quickly get out of hand in a small garden.

Cherokees need lots of cane room. They can shoot up to 20 feet in height and spread just as wide. Their thick, arching canes (I have seen some as thick as my thumb) arch and then sprawl into tangled masses. This can make pruning an unpleasant, not to mention painful, experience, so I can't imagine why anyone would want to force them into 6-foot shrubs. Although it can be done, it seems like self-inflicted torture.

Cherokee roses prefer full sun but will tolerate partial shade. However, in such situations, they will work their way into a nearby tree in an effort to catch more sunlight. This might be worth considering before planting one.

If I had enough room, I'd grow at least a Cherokee rose specimen. If I had plenty of space, a bank of three or five of them, planted at a comfortable distance from well-traveled areas, would look simply grand. Their fragrant, five-petaled, white, waxy blooms with golden yellow stamens put on a spectacular show. Although not repeaters, the 4–5 inch flowers will sometimes show up again in the fall if environmental conditions are right. Depending on your climate, the flowers should appear in late March, April, or May. I have seen the blooms last into early to mid-June at my Charleston friends down the street. Unless you live in the higher elevations where it drops to –3 degrees in the wintertime, these glossy evergreen plants should offer you year-round pleasure.

Cherokee Roses are not finicky about soil conditions. Propagate by cuttings. USDA Hardiness Zones 7–10. AHS Heat Zones 9–3.

Noisette 'Blush'

Rosa x *noisettiana*

Perennial

Noisette 'Blush'
Rosa x *noisettiana*

My Master Gardener buddy was so resolute about me not acquiring a Cherokee Rose that she gave me a cutting of her Noisette 'Blush' a month before the recommended propagation time. USDA Hardiness Zone 8 gardeners usually wait until October to take soft-wood rose cuttings. By then temperatures are usually a little kinder to rootless and almost leafless stems, which are incapable of taking in water for about six weeks. That's about how long it takes before the roots begin growing at those former petiole and thorn sites. But as far as she was concerned, this was an emergency case.

I filled a small, 4-inch-diameter clay pot with a seed starter potting mix of sphagnum peat moss and vermiculite, then poked a hole in the center with a pencil. After snipping off the lower petioles and gently scraping at a thorn or two, I dusted the wounds and the end of the stem with RooTone® rooting hormone. I carefully put about 1 1/2 inches of my 5-inch cutting down the pencil hole. Because I didn't want to shake off the RooTone®, I gently pushed the soil around the stem then soaked the pot in warm water instead of pouring it from a watering can. Then I had to come up with a way to trap as much moisture as possible around the cutting until it took root. Many gardeners use a plastic bag for this purpose, but I have had the unfortunate experience of having wet, drooping ones spoil carefully collected specimens. A rigid cover lessens the risk of leaf or stem rot. It turns out that a 32-ounce, straight-sided, plastic mayonnaise jar fits just inside a 4-inch-diameter pot.

My next assignment was to find a hospitable spot for this cutting. It had to be in a location with a moderate temperature and away from direct sunlight. Knowing that I have a horticultural defect called "out-of-sight-out-of-mind," I knew this little Noisette had to be seen every day or it would never survive.

A little more than a month later, I finally got up the nerve to remove the plastic cover and gently tug on the stem. If the plant had rooted, there should be some resistance. Not long after that, the stem began sprouting new growth. When the canes started getting in our way, I would move the pot to the piazza on warm, sunny days. The rest of the time it sat on a corner of the dining room table.

As long as Noisettes receive good drainage, they could care less about soil requirements. Although the area along my fence is mostly sandy loam, it is not exactly hospitable. The earth is mixed with pebbles, pieces of old bricks, and 1–inch thick tree roots. It was tough work breaking though the first few inches of soil and removing a 2-foot tall sabal palmetto took up the better part of a spring afternoon. My Noisette 'Blush' was not going to be planted in one of those nutrient-rich, carefully tilled, fifty-dollar holes. All it was going to get was a 2-foot-wide, 1-foot-deep home. I was tired, the ax needed sharpening again, and it was starting to get chilly. After several months of pampering, this Noisette was tipped out of its pot, plopped in the ground, and tied to the fence. I threw some 50-0-50 slow release fertilizer at it, raked some live oak leaves around it, gave it some water, and left it to its own devices. In less than two months it was blooming.

I was not prepared for the deliciously sweet, subtle clove scent of the Noisette 'Blush.' These repeat bloomers will produce almost 2–inch soft pink flowers all year long if it isn't swacked with freezing temperatures. However, don't expect constant bloom. It blooms, rests, and then begins the cycle again. Like any flowering plant, deadheading will encourage more blossoms. Since the Noisette flowers hang in clusters, I have found that snipping each spent flower is too time consuming. If you can stand a few spent ones, wait until the entire cluster needs removing.

I have read that Noisette 'Blush' can put out as many as twenty flowers to a cluster. Mine are definitely more plentiful in the spring and summer but I have never counted more than a dozen or so to a cluster. This is probably because my friend receives mostly filtered sunlight and very little full sun. However, the abundance or lack of sun does not affect flower color. Noisette 'Blush' is noted for its deep pink flower buds that turn to the palest of pinks when fully open. It has been my observation that cooler temperatures make the blossoms slightly more pink than summertime ones.

The only complaint that I have about Noisette 'Blush' is that it's often too appealing to unsuspecting admirers. They will rush up to admire the blossoms and breathe in that marvelous scent, forgetting it's a rose and that roses have thorns. I have had to untangle several unsuspecting victims. Perhaps I should put up as sign that says, "Please don't hug the roses."

Propagate by cuttings. USDA Hardiness Zones 6–9. AHS Heat Zones 9–3.

Noisette 'Blush'
Rosa x *noisettiana*

Tropical Plants

There are approximately two hundred species in the hibiscus genus and many of them are defined as shrubs or, at the very least, shrubby perennials. Sometimes I think the latter is a botanical catchall for we-haven't-decided-what-they-truly-are-yet.

Hibiscus spp.

H. acetosella	red shield hibiscus or red hibiscus
H. coccineus	Texas star or red mallow
H. moscheutos	swamp hibiscus or rose mallow
H. mutabilis	Confederate rose
H. rosa-sinensis	Chinese hibiscus or tropical hibiscus

All hibiscuses require full sun and lots of moisture. Guaranteed good drainage is an absolute must for many of them, especially the ever-popular Chinese or tropical hibiscus (*H. rosa-sinensis*).

Hibiscus is a member of the *Malvaceae* family, which includes other plants such as hollyhocks (*Alcea rosea*) and okra (*Abelmoschus esculentus*). This is important to remember because not all hibiscus-looking flowers belong in the hibiscus genus. It is also worth noting that relying on common names to find information about a particular kind of hibiscus doesn't always work. Too many frustrating hours have been lost searching rose books (*Rosa* spp.) for growing information on Confederate roses (*H. mutabilis*). They are not remotely related.

Red shield hibiscus or red hibiscus
Hibiscus acetosella
Tender perennial

Once you have seen *Hibiscus acetosella*, it's easy to understand why one of its common names is red shield hibiscus. The maple-leaf-shaped, reddish green leaves are outlined in dark red. Although some consider their flowers insignificant next to their stunning leaves, don't underestimate their attractiveness. The 2-inch dark magenta flowers begin blooming from the leaf axils about the time our scorching hot weather begins to wane. The flowers provide additional depth and texture to an already handsome plant.

Red shield hibiscus is a very robust hot-weather plant. If left untouched, its upright growth habit can reach 6 feet in USDA Hardiness Zones north of 9 and up to 10 feet tall in southern Florida. A vigorous grower, it likes to be pruned and will not balk if cut almost to the ground a couple of times during the growing season. It is also salt tolerant, which makes it a good beach plant. Just remember that, when not kept at a moderate height, it might get whipped around in strong sea breezes.

The only things that make this hibiscus unhappy are shade and not enough water. In fact, the more sun it receives, the deeper and vibrant the colors. If deprived of moisture, this plant will droop and shed its leaves. Although this survival tactic will rattle many gardeners, it should perk up after a thorough soaking.

There are several cultivars of red shield hibiscus. The name 'red maple' speaks for itself. It looks like a squat, shrubby, red sugar maple (*Acer saccharum*). 'Maple Sugar'PPAF is an improved version of 'red maple.' Dark magenta flowers begin to appear against red to purple tinged leaves in late summer. 'Maple Sugar'PPAF is recommended for USDA Hardiness Zones 9–11, but folks in Zone 8 shouldn't rule it out. Grow one in a large container and overwinter it in a place that never goes below 28 degrees or turn it loose as an accent in a flower bed and treat it as an annual. Other varieties suitable for borders or containers include 'black magic' and 'purple passion.' 'Copper leaf' has softer colored leaves. The usual red is washed to a coppery tone.

Red shield hibiscus blooms in early autumn, about the same time as Confederate roses (*H. mutabilis*). Propagate from cuttings taken from new growth anytime. Some seeds may germinate in situ, or you can collect dried seeds and plant them indoors three months before the last frost. Soaking in warm water for 24 hours before planting encourages germination. Seeds germinate in soil temperatures of 75–80 degrees. USDA Hardiness Zones 9–11. AHS Heat Zones 12–1.

Red shield hibiscus or red hibiscus
Hibiscus acetosella

Texas star or red mallow
Hibiscus coccineus

Texas star or red mallow
Hibiscus coccineus
Herbaceous perennial

The Texas star hibiscus (*H. coccineus*) is native to Georgia's and Florida's swamps and marshes. Its vibrant red, 6–8-inch flower petals are more open or star-shaped than other hibiscus blossoms. This showy plant can grow up to 8 feet tall with a 3–4-foot spread and, because its leaves are narrow and palmate, some think the overall appearance, sans flowers of course, is reminiscent of *cannabis sativa*. Each blossom lasts only one day but the overall bloom is continuous throughout summer and fall.

For gardeners who have an annoying damp spot in their landscape, Texas star might be worth considering. It will even tolerate bouts of extended flooding. Just keep in mind that, in order for it to achieve its signature robust bloom, it must receive full sun or mostly full sun with a bit of partial shade. For those who don't have continually moist soil but are tired of using oleander (*Nerium oleander*) as filler until something else better comes along, *H. coccineus* doesn't mind customary garden soil. It can grow to 7 feet tall in one growing season and ignores sandy soils or ones with too much clay. It could care less about pH. The only thing it doesn't like is salt. But before you rip out that evergreen oleander and plant an uneven number of Texas star 24–36 inches apart, it should be noted that freezing temperatures will cause *H. coccineus* to die back to the ground, even though it reappears in the spring.

Although this is a southeastern native, Texas star is not pest free. Grasshoppers spoil blossoms by chewing on buds and stalk borers can also be a problem. However, no chemical control is usually needed or suggested.

Texas star has a moderate to fast growth rate. Propagate by division in the spring. It often self-seeds from seeds that were dropped during the previous autumn. Texas star is often considered a passalong plant so finding it in a garden center might not be successful. However, a cultivar named 'Lord Baltimore' is often available. Its flowers are deep red. USDA Hardiness Zones 7–9. AHS Heat Zones 12–1.

H. COCCINEUS

When two plant species are crossed, the desirable qualities from each parent suppress the undesirable ones. This is called hybrid vigor, and plant breeders are always looking for new combinations to get it. Plant Delights Nursery in Raleigh, North Carolina, has introduced a new Texas star hybrid named Hibiscus 'Red Flyer.' It's a cross between *H. coccineus* and another native, swamp rose mallow (*H. grandiflorus*). 'Red Flyer' (*H. coccineus* x *H. grandiflorus*) has the swamp rose mallow's good trait for insect resistance while the showy foliage and flower form come from the Texas star.

'Red Flyer' can reach 12 feet in height. It grows best in full sun, prefers moisture, and is a heavy feeder. Expect it to start blooming in mid-July, clear through until first frost. This plant will not self-seed because it is sterile. USDA Hardiness Zones 6–9. AHS Heat Zones 12–1 (estimated)

Swamp hibiscus or rose mallow
Hibiscus moscheutos
Perennial

Rose mallow (*H. moscheutos*) is another southeastern native that thrives around wet areas as long as the soil is well drained and it receives lots of sun. It's a fast grower and is easily propagated from seed, cuttings, or division. Perhaps that's why it has been bred so much. It is used as one of the parents for "dinner plate" hibiscuses, so named because the blossoms are huge—often the size of standard tableware. The flowers are usually varying shades of pink, red, and white. The old-fashioned cultivars such as 'Disco Belle Mix' and 'Southern Belle' sport

Swamp hibiscus
or rose mallow
Hibiscus moscheutos

blossoms up to 12 inches in diameter. (The true wildflowers have blossoms only half that size.) This multi-stemmed, shrubby perennial usually reaches 5 feet in height.

The trend now is to breed shorter, more compact varieties with smaller flowers. 'Fireball'[PP 13,631] and 'Super Rose' are good examples. 'Fireball'[PP 13,631] grows to only 4 feet tall and sends out delicately textured leaves that occasionally display a purple to bluish green tinge. Its deep red, 10-inch flowers bloom from mid-summer to mid-fall. Although it looks terribly tropical, swamp hibiscus is more cold hardy than other varieties and should pull through winters as far north as lower USDA Hardiness Zone 4. Depending on its geographical location in the southeast, 'Super Rose' will grow between 3 and 5 feet with an equal spread. The pink flower size varies from 6 to 12 inches. It is also cold hardy.

If interesting foliage is a prerequisite, 'Red Shield' and 'Kopper King'[PP 10,793] sport shades of burgundy or purple leaves, respectively.

Confederate rose
Hibiscus mutabilis
Perennial

I have had a love-hate relationship with *Hibiscus mutabilis* for many years. It's not entirely the plant's fault, although its propensity for insect problems and powdery mildew doesn't win it any horticultural stars in my book. The first time I saw one of these shrubby, sometimes treelike perennials, was on the College of Charleston campus. This lanky, bobbing-in-the-breeze plant looked strangely out of place among azaleas, live oaks, and crepe myrtles.

Did you ever make those silly toilet tissue flowers when you were in grade school? One stacked copious amounts of 2-plys together, folded them up like an accordion, and tied the center with thread. Then the papers were separated and fluffed to make a pom-pom. Of course, as eight-year-olds we thought these creations were incredibly beautiful, especially if someone could manage to collect different colors of paper. (Need I mention that this fad drove our mothers nuts?) Picture then a 12-foot-tall, spindly shrub with leaves reminiscent of a sycamore tree covered with lots of pink, white, and rose "toilet tissue" flowers. This is what Confederate rose looks like.

Confederate rose
Hibiscus mutabilis

As far as I'm concerned, this plant's only significant horticultural attribute is its ability to display different colors of flowers at the same time, which leads me to my next lament about this peculiar perennial.

Purple heart
Setcreasea purpurea

Folks in the Deep South call *H. mutabilis* "Confederate Rose." The story goes that its flowers turn from white to dark rose in tribute to fallen Confederate soldiers. I have heard perfectly sane gardeners babble on about "getting to the truth" of this plant's folklore. I knew a research librarian who spent hundreds of hours trying to figure out if its name is attributable to a specific event or person. She found nothing.

Although the Southern symbolism behind the Confederate rose may be tearfully poetic and terribly charming, why isn't anyone curious about *how* these plants change flower color? My guess is that most people nonchalantly assume that the color change is similar to the one associated with hydrangeas. Vary the soil pH and the flower color will change accordingly. However, this is not the case with *H. mutabilis.*

As Confederate rose petals mature, they make a pigment called anthocyanin. It's the same one found in other plants, including red roses (*Rosa* spp.), Purple heart (*Setcreasea purpurea*), and even blue cornflowers (*Centaurea cyanus*). (Color hue variations depend on how many anthocyanin molecules are present and how they are arranged.) With Confederate roses, however, the chemistry is a little more complex. When the flowers first begin to open they are white because the scarlet-colored anthocyanin is missing. But as the flower cells begin to age, anthocyanin production kicks in and eventually masks the original white color. The oldest flowers contain the most anthocyanin and are, therefore, the darkest shade of pink.

I have seen blooming Confederate roses so short that they couldn't put up a respectable fight against a zinnia and some brutes tall enough to be called trees. When cultivated along the milder southeast coast, new growth will appear in the spring from old wood. However, gardeners further north or inland shouldn't panic when winter temperatures cause Confederate roses to die back. They will come back from the base of the plant the following spring.

Confederate roses not grown in mostly shade are usually spindly and will flop over in thunder or tropical storm strength winds. (They are also the ones who are most susceptible to white fly, mealy bugs, aphids, and powdery mildew.) If Confederate roses are annually pruned within six weeks of the last bloom-fade, they will grow into much sturdier and healthier plants. However, snipping a blooming branch or two for enjoyment indoors is certainly not discouraged. Pruning in the dead of winter, no matter how much the plant displeases your sense of horticultural good order, should be avoided. Severe cold (*i.e.*, 25 degrees or below) will kill freshly exposed, tender plant growth. The damage from such situations can extend down into the limb from the pruning cut. If the opportunity for late autumn/early winter pruning was missed, wait until there are about two weeks of nonfreezing temperatures before cutting back extraneous growth.

I have been told that Confederate roses are extremely easy to propagate in spring or fall. Simply cut off a 12–18-inch section of a thick-as-a-pencil stem, strip off the lower leaves and place in a 3:1 mixture of moist sand and peat. I must confess that I am a Charlie Brown when it comes to getting a Confederate rose to root. I have never been able to get the stupid things to root. I have even been given cuttings by well-meaning friends who have assured me that "feet" will appear in no time if I just put the stems in a glass of water. They say it's as easy as flying a kite.

Most of the Confederate roses I have seen growing in Charleston's historic district have double 3–5-inch flowers. There are single ones that display typical hibiscus flower characteristics and have the same diameter as the double ones. Both types eventually develop hairy capsules that contain fuzzy seeds, which is why some call this plant cotton flower.

Confederate roses are often considered passalong plants, so they might be difficult to find. However, a variety named 'Rubra,' with double pink flowers that turn to red, is sometimes available as well as 'Flora Plena'. USDA Hardiness Zones 7–10. AHS Heat Zones 12–1.

Chinese or tropical hibiscus
Hibiscus rosa-sinensis
Annual and perennial

Chinese or tropical hibiscus *Hibiscus rosa-sinensis*

Why is it that the showiest, most desirable plants are the ones that cause us the most heartache? Chinese hibiscus (*Hibiscus rosa-sinensis*) may be wildly popular, mainly because their showy flowers come in every imaginable shade and color except blue, but it can be troublesome to grow. Aphids, whiteflies, and Japanese beetles top the list and leaf drop is also a concern.

The key to growing healthy Chinese hibiscus is to plant them in a spot that fits *their* requirements, not the gardener's. In other words, horticultural control freaks won't win over many tropical hibiscuses. If I seem a tad too cranky about *H. rosa-sinensis/Homo sapiens* relationships, please forgive me. I long ago accepted my position as a Chinese hibiscus arbitrator for hundreds of these over-loved yet misunderstood plants. Such is the fate of most Deep South county extension service Master Gardeners.

I have seen Chinese hibiscus thriving in some of the craziest places around Charleston, so I have come to the conclusion that these plants do best when they are not pampered. Who would ever imagine that these deep green, glossy-leaved shrubs with 6–8-inch colorful blossoms could find happiness growing in about 8 inches of soil between a foundation and an asphalt alley? They bloomed all summer and well past Thanksgiving. Another magnificent specimen spent its time waving to passersby while perched on top of a little knoll at a busy intersection. The additional elevation plus heavy mulching protected it from the extremes of too much water and infrequent irrigation. I watched all of these plants for several months waiting to see if they would acquire the usual maladies so many gardeners worry about. It never happened.

When Chinese hibiscus leaves turn yellow and fall off, it's either from aphids sucking the life out of them or the plant is in desperate need of water. The good news is that once these ailments are corrected, new leaves quickly appear. However, if an aphid-ridden plant isn't completely debugged, these soft-bodied insects will probably come charging back with a vengeance because they just love tender new growth.

Insects such as Japanese beetles, whiteflies, or aphids can be difficult to get rid of. There are commercial products for such intrusions, but read the instructions on the label and then follow them. Please don't spray more often than recommended or increase the dosage. I have heard too many sad stories about killing Chinese hibiscuses with kindness.

In USDA Hardiness Zones 9–11, these plants are perennials and can be planted during any time of the year. When they are growing in a year-round tropical environment, like at the southern end of Florida, they can grow up to 12 feet tall with a spread of 6–10 feet. In all the other cold hardiness zones, they must be treated as annuals and will reach about half that size in height and spread. No matter where they live, Chinese hibiscuses must be respected for their semitropical bent. A direct hit of 32 degree ambient air will assuredly turn them to toast.

Gardeners who can't bear to part with their plants during the winter months will be relieved to know that Chinese hibiscus happily adjusts to indoor living if given sufficient natural sunlight. Prune them in March and propagate by taking cuttings in September. Most *H. rosa-sinensis* seed will not come true so expect to be disappointed. However, for the perpetually curious, seeds should sprout in soil temperatures of 75–80 degrees and soaking in warm water for 24 hours before planting encourages germination.

Chinese hibiscus is considered a perennial in USDA Hardiness Zones 9–11. The rest of us will have to treat them as annuals. Propagate with cuttings. AHS Heat Zones 12–1.

Chinese or tropical hibiscus
Hibiscus rosa-sinensis

Shrimp Plant

Justica brandegeana   **Shrimp plant**
Pachystachys lutea   **Yellow shrimp plant,**
                               Golden shrimp plant

Although shrimp plant (*Justica brandegeana*) and yellow shrimp plant (*Pachystachys lutea*) have different botanical names, they are closely related cousins. Both belong to the *Acanthaceae* family. Their botanical difference, aside from bract color, has to do with pollen and stamen characteristics. However, this is a technical issue and not one for gardeners to worry about.

Shrimp plant
Justica brandegeana

Shrimp plants may not be to everyone's liking because their floral effect is hardly conventional. They sport colorful bracts that look frighteningly similar to the crustaceans that Charlestonians zealously eat with stone-ground grits. In addition to this peculiar trait, snow-white flowers emerge from carapace-looking bracts, so the overall result is similar to shaggy shrimp attached to stems and leaves. However, the color play between the colorful bracts, white flowers, and oval foliage is impressive and, when shrimp plants are planted in masses, they can make quite a statement.

For gardeners who are still not sold on these weirdoes, would it help if you knew that, when it comes to taking heat and humidity, these are very tough cookies? What if someone told you that shrimp plants usually bloom from spring through summer and are hummingbird magnets? Naturally, vegetation this perfect must come with at least one caveat. Scale and spider mites can at times be a nuisance, but I certainly wouldn't exclude shrimp plants from my garden over such a minor detail.

Shrimp plant and yellow shrimp plant are usually sold generically (*i.e.*, there are no named varieties or cultivars).

Shrimp plant
Justica brandegeana
Annual and perennial
Shrimp plant (*J. brandegeana*) is a tropical, very frost-sensitive plant. Although it can be grown as a perennial anywhere south of USDA Hardiness Zone 9b, the rest of us will have to grow it as an annual. (Some grow it as a houseplant.) It is prized more for its showy, reddish orange bracts than its oval, light green leaves that can grow up to 2 1/2-feet in length. The inch long, heart-shaped bracts, which are simply modified leaves, overlap themselves in a coat-of-mail fashion. Their gently bending habit resembles the tail end of a shrimp that ever so slightly dangles down from pale green stems. The white tubular flowers appear more as an afterthought than a floral statement and they fade much

quicker than the bracts. These scalelike plant parts can hold their color for several weeks before turning almost black. Once they reach that stage, it is time to deadhead. Some believe that *J. brandegeana's* reddish orange bracts are more robust than *P. lutea's* yellow ones, but I have never read a credible discussion on the subject.

Shrimp plant will reach a height of 2–3 feet. It will grow in part shade and is a heavy feeder. Indulge it with a balanced, liquid fertilizer at half-strength and *J. brandegeana* will reward you with opulent bracts. Frequent pinching will keep this plant from getting too spindly or gangly. Although one would think that a plant named shrimp would enjoy the ocean, neither genus is salt tolerant.

Yellow shrimp plant, golden shrimp plant
Pachystachys lutea
Annual and perennial

Yellow shrimp plant (*P. lutea*) sports showy, 5–6-inch-long, erect bracts that appear to levitate over oval-shaped, 2–4-inch evergreen leaves. (Imagine a shrimp floating at attention.) Gardeners who grow this plant as an annual can expect yellow shrimp plant to reach heights of 3–4 feet with a 2–3-foot-wide spread. However, it can grow as tall as 6 feet in USDA Hardiness Zones 9b–11 and can be used as a hedge as long as one is willing to hard prune almost to the ground once a year. Yellow shrimp plant will get leggy if it is not vigorously cut back. Grow this plant in full sun or part shade.

It too is a heavy feeder and should be given monthly doses of a balanced slow-release fertilizer. Container-grown specimens will benefit from a twice a month drink of half-strength liquid fertilizer. Even the higher octane formulas, such as 20–20–20, that are often not recommended for summertime herbaceous plants, will do it no harm.

Both kinds of shrimp plants can be propagated by cuttings. USDA Hardiness Zones 9b–11. AHS Heat Zones 12–1.

Yellow Shrimp Plant
Pachystachys lutea

Dahlias

In all my years as a Master Gardener with the Charleston County Extension Service, no one has ever asked me a question about dahlias. Perhaps people don't have crises with them on Thursday afternoons between the hours of 1:00 and 4:30, or maybe they are too embarrassed to admit that they try growing them.

'Terracotta' dahlia
D. x *hortensis*
'Terracotta'

Dahlia
Dahlia spp.
Annual or perennial

This is because many Deep South gardeners have been hoodwinked into believing that dahlias have about the same summertime chances of survival as an alpine flower like edelweiss (*Leontopodium alpinun*)—absolutely none. However, I prefer the Dahlia Society of Alabama's more optimistic motto, "Dahlias do grow in the South."

I had never given dahlias much consideration until I fell madly in love with one a few summers ago. Until then I avoided plants that came with instructions such as "lift tubers and overwinter in pots," as well as descriptions that included words like "crown gall," "wilt," and "spray." But after being introduced to an adorable dahlia named 'Terracotta' at Plant Delights Nursery, I began to wonder if the two of us might get through a southeastern summer together with minimal misery. Thus began my quest for the truth about growing dahlias in Dixie.

The common garden dahlia goes by the botanical name *D.* x *hortensis* or *D.* x *variabilis* and is probably a cross between *D. pinnata* and *D. coccinea*. Spanish explorers found both growing in Mexico and shipped them back to the Royal Botanical Gardens in Madrid where a young Swedish scientist named Andreas Dahl was studying. The plant, which was later hybridized throughout Europe, was named for Dahl as a gesture of friendship between the botanical gardens' curator and the Swede.

The dahlia became wildly popular in nineteenth-century Europe because its plump roots, or tubers, were looked upon as a promising food source. The French, including their cattle, turned up their noses at this purported delicacy, while the British successfully passed off dahlia tubers as Jerusalem artichokes. This culinary adventure eventually ended with a whimper but, in the process of trying to invent a better-tasting tuber, the English discovered that dahlia breeding could be quite remunerative. Double-flowered forms were easy to come by and the dahlia was capable of producing every color but blue.

Meanwhile, back in Spain, Madrid's Royal Botanical Gardens had problems with breeding dahlias because they were under the assumption that these plants required a tropical environment. Once the dahlias were let out of the hothouse and planted in more moderate climes, they began to thrive. This is something that some southern gardeners must keep in mind. Although every land grant horticulture school in the Southeast recommends dahlias for home gardens, folks who live in the southernmost regions won't be able to enjoy them during the summer. It's simply too hot for these subtropical plants. Y'all will have to wait and enjoy them in winter and spring.

One of the fun things about growing dahlias is deciding which ones to grow. Because of their incredible ability to breed with one another, the flower head shape and size selection is mind boggling. The American Dahlia Society (www.dahlia.org) recognizes twelve blossom categories: single, anemone, colarette, peony, formal decorative, informal decorative, ball, pompon, incurved cactus, straight cactus, semi-cactus, and miscellaneous. With such a wide selection of flower shapes, plus the fact that dahlia height runs from 6 feet down to 6 inches, it seems almost impossible not to find one that will please even the most finicky gardener.

I will be the first to admit that the exacting horticultural requirements for dahlias may not be for everyone. However, if they are given what they need, dahlias will reward gardeners with breathtaking beauty near the end of summer. I once admired a magnificent specimen that had been planted at the entrance to a James Island, South Carolina, gated community. This plant was part of a commercial landscape scheme, so it received little attention after planting. But someone had placed this dahlia in full sun with plenty of mulch and it bloomed from late July through most of the fall.

Dahlia
D. x *hortensis*

Dahlias are considered both annuals and perennials, depending on where they are grown and if they are overwintered. I'm still not about to dig out and store tubers after the first frost, but planting seed is a reasonable idea for southern gardeners. Seed-grown plants usually stay under 4 feet at maturity. This means that they shouldn't have to be staked like some of their taller, tuber-grown brothers. And some of them are small enough to be planted in containers, which is a plus for gardeners with limited space but want something other than potted petunias for summertime color. No matter where they are grown, dahlias need well-drained soil that is super-rich in organic material. However, skip the manures and high nitrogen fertilizers. You'll end up with more leaves than flowers and if you decide to dig up and store the tubers, they may not be as robust and, therefore, a disappointment the following season. Dahlias prefer a fertilizer that is light on nitrogen (the first number on the package) and rich in phosphorus (second number) and potassium (third number). An often-recommended blend is 5–10–10. Fertilize every three to four weeks until the flowers begin to show, which is usually in late July or early August.

Dahlia seed germinates in 5–20 days at temperatures between 65–70 degrees. Unless the seed packet says otherwise, sow to a depth of 1/16 inch and don't let the potting medium dry out. For gardeners who have older gardening books with dahlia propagation instructions, most cultivars now flower in the first instead of second year and some will produce flowers only a few months after sowing. Another bit of good news is that dahlias transplant easily. Like other plants that have been started indoors, dahlias should be given a chance to acclimatize by gradually letting them adjust to where they will permanently grow.

The following annual cultivar seeds are readily available to home gardeners. Because the botanical names in seed catalogs sometimes differ from company to company, the following nomenclature may differ from the scientifically accepted form.

Dahlias from Seed

Botanical Name	Variety	Flower Type	Color	Height	Flower Size	Exceptional Foliage
D. variabilis	Figaro	Double and semi-double	White	12–14 inches	2 1/2–3 inches	
D. x hybrida (D. pinnata)	Harlequin	Semi-double	White (often with a yellow collar)	12–14 inches	2 1/2 inches	
D. variabilis	Bambino	Single	White with yellow center	12–18 inches	1 inch	Very dark green leaves
D. variabilis	Rigoletto	Double and semi-double	White	15 inches	2 1/2 inches	
D. variabilis	Collarette Dandy	Collarette	White (inner collar has contrasting quilled petals)	20–24 inches	4–6 inches	
D. hortensis	Diablo	Double	Cream	15 inches	2–4 inches	Deep bronze foliage
D. x hybrida (D. pinnata)	Harlequin	Semi-double	Apricot (often with a yellow or white collar)	12–14 inches	2 1/2 inches	Dark green with metallic tinges of purple and black
D. variabilis	Bishop's Children	Single and semi-double	Bronze orange	24–36 inches	2–4 inches	Dark green with metallic tinges of purple and black
D. hortensis	Diablo	Double	Orange	15 inches	2–4 inches	Deep bronze foliage

Dahlias from Seed (continued)

Botanical Name	Variety	Flower Type	Color	Height	Flower Size	Exceptional Foliage
D. variabilis	Rigoletto	Double and semi-double	Orange	15 inches	2 1/2 inches	
D. variabilis	Collarette Dandy	Collarette	Orange (inner collar has contrasting quilled petals)	20–24 inches	4–6 inches	
D. x *hybrida* (*D. pinnata*)	Harlequin	Semi-double	Orange (often with a yellow or white collar)	12–14 inches	2 1/2 inches	
D. variabilis	Double Extreme	Double and semi-double	Orange/yellow	12–24 inches	2–4 inches	
D. variabilis	Bishop's Children	Single and semi-double	Orange/yellow	24–36 inches	2–4 inches	Dark green with metallic tinges of purple and black
D. variabilis	Figaro	Double and semi-double	Pink	12–14 inches	2 1/2–3 inches	
D. hortensis	Diablo	Double	Pink	15 inches	2–4 inches	Deep bronze foliage
D. variabilis	Rigoletto	Double and semi-double	Pink	15 inches	2 1/2 inches	
D. variabilis	Bishop's Children	Single and semi-double	Pink	24–36 inches	2–4 inches	Dark green with metallic tinges of purple and black

Dahlias from Seed (continued)

Botanical Name	Variety	Flower Type	Color	Height	Flower Size	Exceptional Foliage
D. variabilis	Bishop's Children	Single and semi-double	Purple	24–36 inches	2–4 inches	Dark green with metallic tinges of purple and black
D. variabilis	Bishop's Children	Single and semi-double	Garnet	24–36 inches	2–4 inches	Dark green with metallic tinges of purple and black
D. variabilis	Figaro	Double and semi-double	Red	12–14 inches	2 1/2–3 inches	
D. variabilis	Rigoletto	Double	Red	15 inches	2 1/2 inches	
D. hortensis	Diablo	Double	Red	15 inches	2–4 inches	Deep bronze foliage
D. variabilis	Collarette Dandy	Collarette	Red (inner collar has contrasting quilled petals)	20–24 inches	4–6 inches	
D. x hybrida (D. pinnata)	Harlequin	Semi-double	Rose (often with a yellow or white collar)	12–14 inches	2 1/2 inches	
D. variabilis	Rigoletto	Double and semi-double	Rosy purple	13 inches	2 1/2 inches	
D. x hybrida (D. pinnata)	Harlequin	Semi-double	Scarlet (often with a yellow or white collar)	12–14 inches	2 1/2 inches	

Dahlias from Seed (continued)

Botanical Name	Variety	Flower Type	Color	Height	Flower Size	Exceptional Foliage
D. variabilis	Bishop's Children	Single and semi-double	Maroon	24–36 inches	2–4 inches	Dark green with metallic tinges of purple and black
D. variabilis	Redskin	Double and semi-double	Maroon to bronzy green	12–15 inches	2–4 inches	Leaves are tinged with red
D. x *hybrida* (*D. pinnata*)	Harlequin	Semi-double	Violet (often with a yellow or white collar)	12–14 inches	2 1/2 inches	
D. variabilis	Figaro	Double and semi-double	Yellow	12–14 inches	2 1/2–3 inches	
D. hortensis	Diablo	Double	Yellow	15 inches	2–4 inches	Deep bronze foliage
D. variabilis	Rigoletto	Double and semi-double	Yellow	15 inches	2 1/2 inches	
D. variabilis	Collarette Dandy	Collarette	Yellow (inner collar has contrasting quilled petals)	20–24 inches	4–6 inches	
D. x *hybrida* (*D. pinnata*)	Harlequin	Semi-double	Yellow (often with a yellow or white collar)	12–14 inches	2 1/2 inches	

Of course, I know what's going to happen to some gardeners after enjoying their seed-grown-only-meant-to-be-annuals dahlias. They're going to want to keep them for seasons to come and will dig out the tubers after first frost. (For gardeners who are willing to take chances, dahlias will sometimes survive a southern winter if they are given 3–4 inches of loose mulch like pine straw.) Make sure to leave a portion of the old stem attached to the tuber. The new plant needs this stem for bud development. It is best to wait a few days to let the freshly dug tubers dry out before storing them in bags or buckets of vermiculite or clean builders' sand. Store them in a place that does not get colder than the upper 30s and no warmer than 50 degrees. If the tubers later look like they are shriveling, lightly spritz them with water but don't overdo it. Replant dahlia tubers in May or June. If they have survived the winter outdoors, they can be divided once the tuber eyes have sprouted and the new growth is less than 1 inch long.

For gardeners who don't care to fuss with seed, the Dahlia Society of Georgia (www.dahliasocietyofgeorgia.org) offers a list of popular, easy-to-grow, heat-tolerant dahlias. Tubers are readily available at garden centers and from catalogs.

USDA Hardiness Zones 9–11. AHS Heat Zones 9–3.

Buddies
and Bandits

It has been my observation that there are two extremes of gardeners. There are those who approach gardening as a competitive sport and those who contentedly go with the horticultural flow. Most of us are somewhere in the middle. We want our plant selections to be interesting—even unusual—certainly within the bounds of acceptable good taste. But what happens when gardeners become enamored of plants that others call weeds?

Eupatorium spp.

Eupatoriums are sometimes collectively called bonesets. There are approximately 38 plants in this genus and most of them are native to the United States. They are bold, late-summer bloomers with blue to lavender or sometimes white flower heads. Although often ignored in this country as nothing more than big weeds, European gardeners are quite fond of our Eupatoriums.

These perennials prefer full sun but will put up with afternoon shade. Most prefer moist, well-drained soil that is rich in organic material. In general, they are disease free and have few insect problems. Leaf miners are sometimes a nuisance, but cutting off the stems with unsightly leaves is all that is required. Since these plants are prolific growers, periodic pruning and snipping will not sacrifice later bloom.

Mistflower, hardy ageratum
Eupatorium coelestinum

Mistflower, hardy ageratum

Eupatorium coelestinum

I find it curious that many gardeners have adopted the notion that native plants are always good—as if Mother Nature had tenets on botanical morality. Too many of us assume that indigenous plants are always polite and never overstep their boundaries. Ha!

Eupatorium coelestinum, commonly named mistflower, or hardy ageratum, is what one might call the black sheep of the Eupatorium tribe. This native perennial is either loved or hated. There is no middle ground. Don't confuse this plant with the smaller yet similar looking annual named ageratum (*Ageratum houstonianum*). This well-behaved amigo hails from central Mexico, Guatemala, and Honduras.

Mistflowers grow to a height of 1–3 feet and show off fuzzy, bluish lavender flowers in late summer. It populates all of the eastern United States, through West Texas and up into Nebraska. Although it is native, it has managed to hog its way into new territories, thereby becoming a nuisance. Southeastern gardeners who live along the coastal plain might consider the mistflower a weed. It grows along roadsides and moist areas such as ditch banks. It is one of my favorite, late-summer blooming plants.

I suspect that long ago, someone intentionally planted mistflower in our garden because its placement in the landscape is too calculated. However, I encouraged it to grow in a few more places and, at times, I wish I hadn't. Mistflower spreads rapidly by zealous rhizomes. Although rogue plants always yank out quite easily, more are guaranteed to return. The only way to permanently remove these little trespassers is with a spritz of Roundup®.

Except for occasionally thinning out overcrowded spots, as well as pulling out every plant after it has finished blooming in late September or early October, mistflowers are maintenance-free plants. The blossoms don't need deadheading, the plants don't flop over, and I have never seen as much as a hint of disease. They are impervious to accidental mowing, whacking, and trampling. Although they will not grow in soggy soil, they do like damp places and are quite content to inhabit the edge of a bog garden. Wherever they are planted, make sure they are easily accessible in case they get out of control.

Mistflowers' peccadilloes are soon forgotten when they begin to bloom. If planted in masses, their iridescent blue blossoms practically glow in the early morning sun. They are also wonderful foils for other plants and creatures. Shades of yellow, pink, and orange from neighboring blooms appear more vibrant, and bumblebees wearing Georgia Tech sweaters look spectacular against the mistflower's wooly lapis lazuli blue.

Gardeners who prefer orderly border designs should probably skip growing mistflower. However, if held captive in a pot it could add a dramatic, late-summer accent in a formal setting. Transplant small clumps into a container in early spring and pinch back growth every time it reaches 6–8 inches. Turn it loose in early August for bloom in September. USDA Hardiness: zones 5–11. AHS Heat: zones 9–11.

Joe-Pye weed
Eupatorium maculatum
Perennial

For gardeners who desire a little more control over their perennial borders yet desire the casual wildness that native Eupatoriums bring to the landscape, they should consider *Eupatorium maculatum*. No, not the wild version of Joe-Pye weed that can reach 10–15 feet in height (unless one has lots of room) but a tamer variety named 'Gateway' (*E. maculatum* 'Gateway'). Although a little more compact in growth habit than its undomesticated cousin, this cultivar still needs a bit of elbow room. It will grow to 5–6 feet with a 4–6 foot spread. The 12–18-inch lavender or dusky pink blossoms attract butterflies and the seed heads later make an attractive wintertime statement. This version of Joe-Pye weed looks its best when planted at the back of borders or used as a screen. It doesn't mind having wet feet and I have read that it makes a terrific bog garden plant if the soil pH is fairly neutral. Like other members of this tribe, it too blooms in late summer and early fall. Propagate by seeds or division. USDA Hardiness: zone 4–9. AHS Heat: zones 9–11.

Joe-Pye weed
Eupatorium purpureum
Perennial

Will the real Joe-Pye weed please stand up? *Eupatorium purpureum* and *E. maculatum* are both called Joe-Pye weed. This is one of the many reasons why common names drive us nuts: the same appellation for different plants. In this case they are in the same genus.

If an unsuspecting shopper walks into a garden center and requests Mr. Pye, they might have a slim chance of getting what they think they want. And if an unsuspecting retail associate starts tossing out botanical names and expecting a prompt, intelligent answer from the buyer, then chances are that someone will spend the rest of the day with hurt feelings. Fortunately, there are other ways to maneuver around such a nomenclatorial predicament. One can learn additional common names or simply learn how to identify the plant.

The epithet *purpureum* means purple so this species is sometimes called purple Joe-Pye weed or purple boneset because the stems at the joints are tinged with a purplish raspberry color. Others call it sweet Joe-Pye weed because its blossoms emit a smell reminiscent of vanilla. The fuzzy lavender flowers appear in August and September. A popular cultivar, 'Big Umbrella,' has scented, dark lavender blossoms with deep purple stems.

Purple Joe-Pye weed is similar in height and spread to its cousin *E. maculatum*. It prefers moist, well-drained soils but can tough it out during most dry spells. Propagate by division in spring or sow seeds in spring or fall when soil temperatures are a cool 50 degrees. USDA Hardiness: zones 5–9. AHS Heat: zones 9–11.

Joe-Pye

The real Joe Pye can't stand up because he's no longer among us. No, there is no DNA evidence, but a few reliable records might exist; his true identity is based mostly on folklore. An Algonquin medicine man named Joseph Pye supposedly cured a typhus-type fever outbreak in the Massachusetts Bay colony with a plant that looked similar to what we now identify as *Eupatorium maculatum* or *E. purpureum*. The concoction induced the sweats, which in turn cured the illness.

A Mr. Pye was allegedly from Salem, Massachusetts. Records dating c. 1787 suggest that one of his possible descendants, also named Joe Pye, was still living in the area. However, all of this is circumspect and no one has unequivocally documented this story.

Blanket flower

Gaillardia spp.

There are approximately thirty species of *Gaillardia* that are native to North America, but we are only interested in a few of them. Gaillardias are prized for their ability to keep blooming even under the hottest conditions. They look equally fabulous in a border, a vase, or growing along a ditch. (Notice I said growing *along* a ditch, not *in* a ditch.)

Gaillardias need full sun—ideally 6–8 hours of direct light—and well-drained soil. If they are planted in a wet situation, root rot is guaranteed. They are prone to downy mildew and leaf spot if they are exposed to endless rains and relentless bouts of monsoon-type humidity. Leafhoppers consider *Gaillardias* a delicacy.

If you have turned up your nose at these rugged plants because bright red or orange petals tipped with flaming yellow just didn't fit in with your color scheme, then keep reading. Horticulturists and breeders have recently come up with softer hues and one gaillardia is soft pink.

The only difficult part to finding a particular gaillardia for your garden is the redundancy of common names. The genus *Gaillardia* goes by the catchall name "blanket flower" but some of its species go by the same appellation. Sometimes seed catalogs just identify a plant as gaillardia or blanket flower and fail to list the complete botanical name. This can be frustrating to folks who are after a specific plant. For the rest of us who don't need to be so exact, as long as the plant is some kind of gaillardia, we can rest assured that it will end up giving us pleasure.

Blanket flower, gaillardia, fire-flower

G. pulchella

Annual

If I could choose the ideal traveling companions, they would seldom sulk, happily adjust to new situations, and hold up under the most adverse conditions.

Why can't we humans be more like *G. pulchella*? This dependable annual has wandered around the southern half of the United States for so long that we're really not sure where its journey began. The consensus is that it traveled from the Southwest to the Southeast, but that's just an educated guess.

This handsome little wildflower is often called blanket flower or just plain old gaillardia. However, I prefer its Deep South common name, fire-flower, because that best describes its 2-inch, dark orange, sunflowerlike blossoms that are tipped with bright yellow. Its outer corolla is reminiscent of a ring of fire. This bold little plant has managed to multiply along the southeastern seaboard's beach dunes and roadsides. Since it prefers sandy soils, it shouldn't surprise anyone that it's drought tolerant.

Of course, a plant this showy just had to be captured and domesticated. Blanket flowers have been selectively bred to create bolder colors and frillier petals. If you prefer fancier blossoms, 'Sundance Bicolor' (AAS winner 2003) sports multiple shades of orange-colored pom-poms. This variety will reach about 12 inches tall with a 15-inch spread. *G. pulchella* will grow 1–2 feet tall and 2 feet wide. USDA Hardiness Zones 3–11. AHS Heat Zones 12–1.

Blanket flower
G. aristata
Perennial

Another *Gaillardia* species, *G. aristata*, also thrives throughout much of the United States. It too is appreciated for its drought tolerance as well as that signature fiery glow along its outer yellow rings. But if you prefer red petals to orange ones, this plant is for you. For a while, *G. aristata* fell out of favor with gardeners because a newcomer, *G. aristata*, was crossed with *G. pulchella* to create *Gaillardia* x *grandiflora* and it upstaged all the other gaillardias for many years. However, it's fortunate that we finally returned to our senses. *G. aristata* seeds easily, thrives in full sun, and makes a splendid plant for drainage ditch slopes. The folks at Texas A & M say that 1 ounce of *G. aristata* seed will cover

272 square feet, which is about a 16 x 16-foot plot. Plant *in situ* when soil temperatures reach 70-75 degrees and just barely cover with 1/8 inch of soil. In about 15 to 45 days, you should see signs of life. Expect continual flowering throughout the summer months on plants that grow 1–2 feet tall and 2 feet wide. USDA Hardiness Zones 3–8. AHS Heat Zones 12–1.

Blanket flower
G. x *grandiflora*
Hybrid perennial

Talk about good genes. This plant seems to have it all. It's at home in gardens from USDA Heat Zones 2–10, produces an abundance of blooms over very long periods, and is easy to grow. Its only problem is that one parent, *G. aristata*, is an annual, while the other, *G. pulchella*, is a perennial. Evidently, the annual's chromosomes shorten the overall longevity of the offspring. But don't let an estimated life expectancy of only two years turn you off. In return you get a spectacular plant with 2–3 inch maroon flowers tipped with yellow and a dark purple to burgundy center. The fun part about this plant is that it's full of surprises. Most of its cultivars can be grown from seed and there's a great deal of color variation because of its hybridity. And unlike some seed-grown perennials that underperform during their first season, these plants will definitely produce flowers during their first year. This blanket flower version will grow to 2–3 feet tall with a 2-foot spread. Dwarf varieties are also available (most stay under 12 inches tall), but two of the more sought-after varieties, 'Baby Cole' and 'Goblin', are propagated from cuttings, not seed. USDA Hardiness Zones 2–10. AHS Heat Zones 12–1.

White firewheel
G. aestivalis var. *winkleri*

This is one of those plants that, after we find out about it, we desperately, passionately want but will probably never have. It's an endangered species, which means that federal laws make its propagation and sales to the public extremely difficult. Plant Delights Nursery, Inc. in North Carolina makes a pinkish version available, but only during their open houses. They cannot ship this plant to you and seeds are not available. Now, before you accuse owner Tony Avent of plantnapping, his nursery received white firewheel cuttings from the renowned American horticulturist, J. C. Raulston (1940–1996).

White firewheels are only found growing wild in one county in southeastern Texas. Instead of the characteristic red, orange, and yellow petals, these beauties sport solid colors of white to dark plum with yellow to purple centers. If you wish to see these plants, the Mercer Botanical Gardens in Humble, Texas, grows them in their Endangered Species Garden. In the meantime, the University of Georgia's 2005 trial gardens, The Gardens at UGA, has cultivated a firewheel variety named *G. aestivalis* var. *winkleri* 'Homestead Pink with Yellow Center.'

If you are as charmed by *G. aestivalis* var. *winkleri* as I am, my only suggestion is to watch plant and seed catalogs for this species. I predict that it will someday become readily available. Instead of asking, "Why wasn't I told about this before?" you will know about it before it reaches the marketplace.

The 'Homestead Pink with Yellow Center' received a Gardens at UGA rating of 4.38 out of a perfect score of 5. Athens, Georgia is in AHS Heat Zone 8. Tony Avent has placed *G. aestivalis* var. *winkleri* in USDA Hardiness Zones 7–9 although he surmises that this variety might survive temperatures slightly lower than zero degrees. USDA Hardiness Zones 7–9 (estimated). AHS Heat Zones 12–1 (estimated).

Oranges and Lemons
Gaillardia x *grandiflora*

Gaillardia

I was once given two young *Gaillardia* x *grandiflora* cultivars named 'Oranges and Lemons' (PPAF). It was mid-July and I didn't know what to do with them because it was just too hot to think about it. One of the 2-inch pots got knocked over in a thunderstorm and the poor fellow eventually died of thirst. I felt guilty about my neglect and decided that it was time to plant the lone survivor. When I dashed inside to grab the planting information, I discovered that 'Oranges and Lemons' had been bred and tested in the United Kingdom. Botanically speaking, there are indeed times when our southeastern-growing climate is very similar to England's, but the height of summer definitely isn't one of them. I figured that this plant would soon be joining its brother in the compost heap.

Out of desperation, I finally stuck this scraggly plant in a large container that was already home to way too many garden mums and a bushy volunteer vinca that I had failed to evict. It was the hottest part of the day, so I threw a bucket of water on this pathetic transplant and wished it good luck. About ten days later 'Oranges and Lemons' started blooming. It eventually stopped producing buds when the hoggish mums intruded. The restricted sunlight had also made him spindly. All it needed was a little more space, so I clipped and pushed away some of the offending vegetation. By mid-September he had gathered enough energy to start blooming again. I loved him for his determination.

Lantana and Verbena

When I first moved to Charleston, gardeners thought that lantana (*Lantana camera*) was a junk plant and verbena (*Verbena* spp.) was a weed. My, how times have changed! Lantana and verbena have become the rage throughout the Southeast and folks further north are now demanding their fair share. As a result, breeders are scrambling to create more cold-hardy lantanas to satisfy gardeners in USDA Hardiness Zone 7 and further north who want them as perennials instead of annuals.

Verbena has progressed from a plant that was associated with faded gentility to a grand, upscale position. In some neighborhoods, it has become a contest to see who can find the latest, most colorful cultivar. And, when the first bright yellow varieties of lantana were introduced several years ago, stories of garden thefts became a popular subject at parties.

Because of their strikingly similar attributes, it's not uncommon to hear gardeners confess that they cannot distinguish lantana from verbena. Relax. This is to be expected. These plants are almost kissing cousins. They are both from the Vervain family, have hairy, square stems (it's sometimes easier to feel the squareness than to see it) and similar-looking flower heads. When they are grown in full sun, they add color to any garden.

Lantana

Lantana spp.
Lantana camera

Annual or perennial

I have friends who would rather grow kudzu than lantana (*Lantana camera*). I have to confess that it would never make my plants-to-buy list but, on the other hand, I have never considered getting rid of the ones that came with our property. We enjoy watching the flower-head colors change from light pink and pale yellow in early summer to dark, fiery orange and bright yellow by fall. Butterflies and bees swarm to these bushy, shrublike plants and anoles snooze in them.

As far as I'm concerned, lantana is practically maintenance free. Some gardeners will warn you about lantana lace bugs that ruin leaves and make plants unattractive. Others complain of root rot and powdery mildew. My only annoyance is their scratchy, almost prickly stems and leaves. If lace bugs become a problem, simply cut out the damaged vegetation, then get rid of it. Lantana is a fast grower and will quickly bounce back to its former size. Wearing long sleeves and gloves for this chore is highly recommended. As for disease

Lantana
Lantana camera

Lantana
Lantana camera

issues, they can be avoided by planting lantana where *it* needs to be and not where the gardener *thinks* it should be. Lantanas need full sun, and well-drained soil. Don't worry about soil type. Although newly planted lantanas need lots of water before they adjust to their new surroundings, they are drought tolerant. They also make great beach plants because of their indifference to salt.

Master Gardeners receive plenty of inquiries about lantana. Many wonder what to do with those shiny black seeds. First of all, don't eat them; they are poisonous! Prune out lantana stems whenever seeds begin to appear. They start out green and are about the size of BBs. Some find the seeds annoying, but sterile lantana cultivars are now available (refer to chart below).

Some questions about lantana occur in winter. These plants are very cold sensitive and their leaves will turn a shriveled gray at 32 degrees. For those who have never seen a frost-bitten lantana, they look simply awful. However, removing dead stems should be a springtime chore and never performed in the dead of winter. They are protecting the plant from further damage and removing them might trigger a burst of premature new growth. After the last predicted frost date, lantanas should be severely pruned and dead wood should be removed. When winters are colder than usual, lantanas are sometimes slow to wake up in spring. Don't be too concerned if the plant takes several weeks to send out green shoots after pruning.

Of course, many gardeners still don't give a hoot about my old-fashioned *L. camera* variety. They want to know about the newer cultivars that also laugh at high heat and humidity. The following list is hardly inclusive. Instead it is more of an introduction to the hundreds of varieties that are available. They are listed by height.

Lantana Cultivars

Cultivar	Habit	Color	Height	Spread	Sterile
L. camera 'Patriot Cowboy'	low spreading	Orange and yellow	1 foot	1 foot	No
L. camera 'Patriot Popcorn'	weeping habit	White and yellow	1 foot	2 feet	No
L. camera 'Clear White'	low spreading	White	1-2 feet	4 feet	
L. camera 'Patriot Honeylove'	spreading, slightly mounded with weeping habit	Yellow	2 feet	3 feet	No
L. camera 'New Gold'	low grower	Yellow	2 feet	4 feet	Yes
L. camera 'Samantha' ('Lemon Swirl')	variegated low-grower	Yellow	2-3 feet	4 feet	
L. camera 'Athens Rose'	upright mound	Magenta, rose, pink, yellow	3 feet	4 feet	No
L. trifolia 'Lavender Popcorn'	low grower	Lavender	2–3 feet	2–3 feet	No
L. camera 'Radiation'	tall upright	Orange and yellow	4-5 feet	4-5 feet	No
L. camera 'Patriot Dean Day Smith'	tall upright	Pink, yellow, apricot	6 feet	5 feet	No
L. camera 'Miss Huff'	tall upright	Orange, coral, gold	6-8 feet	6-10 feet	Yes
L. camera 'Mozelle'	upright	Yellow, peach, pink	6-8 feet	6-8 feet	Yes

Propagate by cuttings. USDA Hardiness Zones (7)8–11). AHS Heat Zones 12–1.

Verbenas
Garden verbena
Verbena spp.
Verbena venosa (*V. rigida*)
V. x *hybrida*

V. speciosa 'Imagination'

My interest in verbena began many years ago when a friend inquired about verbena's aroma. This came about because he was reading William Faulkner's *An Odor of Verbena* (from *The Unvanquished*). "What does verbena smell like?" he asked. I didn't have an answer but, since I was going through my let's-grow-plants-mentioned-by-southern-writers stage, I thought solving this mystery would be great fun.

I found a seed catalog that specialized in fragrant plants and promptly ordered their only selection of verbena seed, *V. venosa*. If I remember correctly, the seeds germinated quickly and, within a few months, I had dark, day-glow magenta verbena flower heads nodding in our front border. The only problem was that they lacked fragrance. The offspring from the original seeds have lived in that bed for more than 10 years and not once have I detected even a hint of scent.

Shortly after my carefully tended *V. venosa* began blooming, I was flipping through a weed identification book and found my flowers in a Most Wanted mug shot. Good grief! I was cultivating a common criminal who even had an alias, *Verbena rigida*. Weed or not, eviction was never considered. I allow them to roam wherever they want and, for the most part, they have remained well behaved. They are one of the first plants to bloom in the spring and I love their vibrant color. Their flower show fades in and out during the summer, partly because I don't like deadheading them. Their leaves are unpleasantly scratchy (no wonder they are called "rigida") and I rarely remember the gardening gloves. I have since discovered that not all verbena leaves are as unpleasant as

Verbena
Verbena rigida

V. venosa's, but some gardeners may find other varieties just as irritating because they are only slightly less rough.

My criminal variety is one tough little species. Those abrasive leaves and stems make excellent defenses against crawling and chewing insects, so their only visitors are drowsy, shy bumblebees. Sometimes venosa's leaves show signs of powdery mildew during mid to late winter, but these are quickly dispensed to the yard waste bag.

I was happy to learn that I'm not the only one smitten with these rugged outcasts. Varieties of *Verbena rigida* (a/k/a *venosa*) are now available. *V. rigida* 'Lilacina' is a bushier form of its parent. *V. rigida* 'Polaris' is a light lavender with a silvery tint. Wouldn't it be fun if someone invented a variety named *V. rigida* 'Felony Anne'?

For those who would like to grow my pet weed, *V. venosa*, make sure the seed is prechilled. If not, the seeds will need to be stratified in the refrigerator for 2 weeks before planting them in a well-drained potting medium at 65 degrees. Sow at a depth of 1/16 inch, making sure that the seed is completely covered. *V. venosa* needs total darkness to germinate. This verbena will germinate in 2 weeks but will sometimes exasperate gardeners by poking around for three months before doing what it is supposed to do.

Propagate by seeds or cuttings. USDA Hardiness Zones 8–10. Treat as an annual in other zones. AHS Heat Zones 12–1.

Garden verbena
V. x *hybrida*
Annual or perennial

Garden verbena (*V.* x *hybrida*) is the plant that first comes to mind when verbena is mentioned to southern gardeners. It grows in bushy, 1-foot-tall, spreading clumps and displays 2-inch-diameter flower heads that come in white, pink, red, blue, lavender, or purple. This plant is a complicated mix of many verbena species, including *V. venosa*. Plantsmen began mixing breeds about thirty years before The Late Unpleasantness (aka The Civil War), so I suspect this is the variety in Mr. Faulkner's story. Some kinds have a pleasant, sweet scent, although never strong enough to waft through the air.

Garden verbenas are prodigious bloomers until summer's heat and humidity finally shut them down. Folks in USDA Hardiness Zones 7 and above usually don't have to worry about this, but the rest of us further south do. However, garden verbena can be planted in the fall in USDA Hardiness Zones 8–11 and, if not swacked by a freeze, will bloom through spring and early summer. For gardeners who can keep these plants growing throughout the summer, garden verbena doesn't need much nitrogen to crank out the colorful clusters of flowerets. Instead, give them a high phosphorus and potassium mix and they will reward you with strong plants.

I have been informed that *V.* x *hybrida* seed is exceedingly difficult to germinate, but why bother? Garden verbena plants that have been grown from cuttings are more robust than seed-born ones. Besides, garden centers carry verbena in abundance and it's fun to watch them compete with one another over the newest colors each spring.

Propagate by seeds (not recommended) or cuttings. USDA Hardiness Zones 8–10. Treat as an annual in other zones. AHS Heat Zones 12–1.

'Imagination'
Verbena speciosa 'Imagination'
Annual and perennial
Verbena speciosa 'Imagination' is the perfect high heat and humidity summertime plant for gardeners in USDA Hardiness Zones 8–11. Its low-growing habit makes it a perfect ground cover. Because the stems amble along the ground and root easily, this is a great plant to use if erosion is a problem. 'Imagination' is indifferent to soil type and is drought resistant. This moderate grower needs full sun to spread and bloom. It is not a heavy feeder, but might require an occasional application of a balanced, slow-release fertilizer.

'Imagination' also looks great in a hanging basket or cascading down a wall. Mass plantings, however, really show off this plant. Its finely dissected leaves enhance the flower color. 'Imagination' is available in shades of dark purple or deep violet blue.

Propagate with cuttings. USDA Hardiness Zones 8–10. Treat as annuals in other zones. AHS Heat Zones 12–1.

Ornamental Peppers

It never fails. No matter how meticulous we are about creating a mixed border, a few empty spaces will always ruin the show. Thank goodness for ornamental peppers (*Capsicum annuum*).

Bolivian rainbow
Capsicum annuum

Ornamental peppers
Capsicum annuum

They can fill those annoying voids with colorful, eye-catching interest. No, I'm not talking about lanky bell peppers or poblanos. Save them for the vegetable garden. Ornamental peppers are bushy annuals that produce lots of small, colorful, erect pods. Some of them have interesting leaves, and one of my favorites sports purple instead of white flowers.

Although ornamental peppers are not grown for consumption, their fruit *is* edible. I mention this not only for the curious gourmand but also as a warning. Some pods are fairly mild while others can be quite hot. The heat factor for ornamental peppers can reach 50,000 Scoville Heat Units, which puts some on par with the Tabasco pepper (*C. frutescens*). For this reason, I hesitate to grow hot ornamental peppers near public thoroughfares. Some might argue that a scorching surprise is fitting for someone who takes what is not theirs. However, some of the colorful pods are just too tempting, especially to a small youngster who views the plants at almost eye level.

One of the easiest ways to spot an ornamental pepper is by its erect fruit. Although they are related to bells, paprikas, and jalapeños, the ancient Mexicans selectively cultivated culinary peppers to dangle down, not up. The reason was quite simple. Birds were less likely to spot a meal if it was hidden under leaves. This is why vegetable garden peppers usually have pendulant fruit.

Ornamental peppers are fairly easy to grow from seed, and most will germinate at around 70 degrees. However, some can be temperamental and will refuse to sprout if the temperature is only slightly too low. A soil thermometer can be a pepper grower's best friend. I have started all sorts of peppers on top of refrigerators and water heaters, as well as in an elaborate, coil-heated seed germination box. As long as the seeds receive steady warmth, they should germinate—even if it's a bit sporadic.

One of the more important things about growing peppers from seed is this: When they are very young, they all look alike. Plant different kinds together and you won't be able to distinguish an ornamental from a bell or a cayenne. This is because the dicotyledons and first true leaves all look exactly the same. Later on, the plant's growth habit might provide a useful hint, but not always. And because almost all pepper flowers are white, color will be of no help. Only the fruit will eventually identify the plant.

My problem with ornamental peppers is that I love the one I'm with. However, my all-time favorite is Bolivian rainbow. The slightly less than 3/8-inch purple flowers are quite striking against its greenish purple leaves. Depending on maturity, the roundish, erect fruits are off-white, beige, yellow, purple, and red. By midsummer Bolivian rainbow is a riot of color with continuous bloom and abundant fruit. Our plant, which grows in a 12-inch pot in mostly dappled summer sun, is quite bushy. An errant morning newspaper struck it when it was quite young. It seemed to shrug off the loss of its topmost growth and quickly filled out again. By December it looked like a 15-inch-tall, heavily decorated Christmas tree. Most of the fruit was bright red.

Bolivian rainbows thrive in hot and humid weather. Like all ornamental peppers, they need well-drained soil that is rich in organic material. They also appreciate an occasional boost from a balanced liquid fertilizer. Plants this prolific use a lot of energy so the additional nutrient helps to keep it producing more peppers.

For those who have had unfortunate experiences growing vegetable garden peppers and are therefore wary of trying ornamental ones, please try to relax. The standard litany of complaints about vegetable garden peppers—looks, size, and abundance of fruit—never comes to the fore with ornamental ones. Perhaps this is because ornamental peppers are more closely related to the ancient wild kind and have, therefore, not had the spunk bred out of them.

Insects can also be a problem with edible peppers. Anyone who has ever grown them has probably encountered aphids, flea beetles, and European corn borers. This is not much of a concern for the ornamental varieties. Yes, signs of flea beetle may appear during late spring or early summer. But I look forward to seeing those miniature buckshot holes appear in the pepper leaves. They signal the return of the acrobatic and carnivorous Carolina anoles (*Anolis carolinensis*), which are sometimes called green anoles. The flea beetles are quickly consumed and the anoles stay around to patrol the garden all summer.

Like all *C. annuums*, ornamental peppers will not survive temperatures below 32 degrees and many, like Bolivian rainbows, will start to look rather tired and worn when nighttime temperatures continually hover in the forties. We haul our favorite potted pepper plants inside whenever a freeze is predicted, but we never let anyone overwinter in the house. It's just not practical for either of us. An exceptionally mild winter meant that our Bolivian rainbow spent most of the winter on the piazza where it received lots of afternoon sun. Once nighttime temperatures moderated into the high fifties, it began producing fruit again.

For gardeners who want a little more texture or visual interest from ornamental peppers, there are cultivars such as 'Medusa' or 'Riot' that produce long, twisted, spiked, thin, 2 1/2-inch pods. There are also varieties with variegated leaves (one ingeniously named 'Variegated') and, for the really daring gardener, 'Black Pearls' leaves evolve from green to black. This 2005 All-American Selection winner displays less than 1-inch, rounded, black fruit that later turns red. And for those who can't get enough of damson-colored plants, everything on 'Explosive Ember' either starts out or will become purple.

Ornamental peppers are usually 12–15 inches tall with about the same spread. If lots of them will be grown together, the general rule is to space them about 24 inches apart. Like their vegetable garden cousins, they need six to

eight hours of sunlight per day. However, ornamental peppers appreciate a respite from the broiling afternoon sun and will not balk much over an abundance of filtered or dappled light.

Bolivian rainbow
Capsicum annuum

Gardeners who live in USDA Hardiness Zones 10 and 11 can grow ornamental peppers as perennials. For the rest of us they are considered annuals. They are heat tolerant in American Horticulture Society Heat Zones 12–3. Propagate with seed.

Angels
and Devils

Wise gardeners are those who can keep their landscaping opinions to themselves. In other words, *De gustibus et de coloribus non disputandum* (Concerning taste and color, do not argue). This is especially true when it comes to brugmansias and daturas. They are either scorned or admired.

Brugmansia spp.	**Angels' trumpet**
Datura spp.	**Devil's trumpet**

I had ignored large plants with mammoth, trumpet-shaped flowers until I discovered that my favorite garden writer, the late Henry Mitchell, admired daturas. Mr. Mitchell was the garden writer for the *Washington Post* when we lived in Virginia and I hung on every word he wrote. So when he suggested that daturas and their very close relatives, brugmansias, were worthy of notice, I began seeking them out. After several years of studying them growing in Charleston, I have come to the conclusion that, although these plants are not for everyone, they can be spectacular in the right setting.

Brugmansias and daturas are related to peppers and tomatoes. All are in the Solanaceae family but every part–every inch–of brugmansia and datura is deadly poisonous. I recall reading that more people die from eating plants in the *Datura* genus than from poisonous mushrooms.

Brugmansias and daturas have similar-looking, trumpet-shaped flowers with connecting flared petals at the widest part. Both were classified *Datura* until the 1970s when brugmansias were reassigned to their own genus, *Brugmansia*. Although many folks still confuse the two, there are obvious differences between daturas and brugmansias. An easy way to distinguish them is that brugmansia flowers point down and datura flowers point up. Daturas are lower growing and somewhat weedy looking while brugmansias are much taller and treelike. Another point of confusion is that some gardeners, as well as a few plant sellers, use the common name angels' trumpet for both genera.

Angels' trumpet
Brugmansia spp.
Annual and perennial

For the past several years I have admired a *B.* x *candida* specimen growing across the street from Charleston's harbor. It softens the corner of a house and is tucked in with a few lower-growing perennials. It is exposed to considerable

sea breezes and I always look for it after thunderstorms, expecting to find it blown over. I'm convinced that its 5 1/2-feet height makes it vulnerable to wind-related disasters. The 12-inch pendulant flowers are sometimes blown to the ground, but even after being knocked around in a tropical storm, this angels' trumpet began blooming again in less than a few weeks. But the truly amazing thing about this brugmansia is that it has survived several winters.

Angels' Trumpet
Brugmansia x *candida*

Angels' Trumpet
Brugmansia

Although they will revolt when temperatures go below 40 degrees, brugmansias are cold hardy in USDA Hardiness Zones 8–10. If their roots do not freeze, they should live to see another spring. (The American Brugmansia and Datura Society states that some brugmansias have even survived Zone 7

winters.) My favorite plant is bucking the longevity odds because someone knew where to plant it. This is a perfect example of what can happen if one takes the time to figure out how weather affects a specific landscape situation. If this brugmansia had been planted just twenty more feet out in the open, too cold of temperatures might have killed it. (I have on occasion seen frost at the edge of the property.) Although the ambient air near a body of water is slightly warmer in winter than further inland (or even a few blocks), this angels' trumpet is shielded against cold blasts of northern air as well as being protected by other plants.

Although I have grown quite fond of this fellow and would certainly hate to see him swacked by a cruel winter, if I owned him I would not take heroic steps to save him. Brugmansias are fast growers and reach maturity quickly. Even a youngster planted after the last predicted frost date should flower during the coming summer months if given what it needs to flourish. Brugmansias are definitely "lots-of" plants. They need lots of water, sun, organic material in well-drained soil, fertilizer, and room to grow. If given all that they need, brugmansias will grow 4–6 feet tall with a 5–6-foot spread.

Most of the brugmansias that I have seen growing in Charleston are *B.* x *candida*. When their flowers begin to open, the petals display a slight yellow tinge before turning white. A double white cultivar is also available (*B.* x *candida* 'Double White'). Brugmansias are notorious for their ability to commingle breeds, but *B.* x *candida*'s parents are probably *B. aurea* and *B. versicolor*, two Peruvian varieties that are also available to home gardeners. The latter's foot-long flowers are reminiscent of oversized Easter lilies, while—like its species name suggests—*B. versicolor* comes in several color choices including yellow, peach, pink, and orange. For those interested in staying on top of new varieties and cultivars, the American Brugmansia and Datura Society, Inc. has a Web site at www.abds.net.

Propagate by cuttings. USDA Hardiness Zones (7)8–10. AHS Heat Zones 12–6 (estimated).

Devil's Trumpet
Datura spp.
Annual

There is something sinister and sexy about daturas. Don't be fooled by their coarse foliage, careless habit, or the ability to nonchalantly poison. Those incredibly alluring blossoms are the stuff for grand opera librettos and Theodore Dressier morality novels. Datura's come-hither, heavily perfumed, trumpet-shaped blossoms are available for one-night stands only. Interested only in trysts with night-flying moths, the blossoms quickly fade at dawn. It's hardly a pleasant sight. Used-up blossoms wither and, by the following day, litter the ground. None of this makes any difference to gardeners. Datura's flamboyant blossoms—from cream-colored to shades of purple—continue to mesmerize us. They have become increasingly popular in southern gardens because they shrug off heat and humidity.

Many daturas hail from the tropical regions of the New World, but one, *D. metel,* comes from southwestern China. This is the species that is frequently offered in garden catalogs. It sprawls wider than its height, which is usually 3–4 feet tall. In late afternoon, large, white, trumpet-shaped flowers begin to open, wafting a lilylike scent. The single-flowered *D. metel* is quite easy to grow as long as it is given shade, but these simple yet elegant flowers are getting harder to find. The devil's trumpets now offered to gardeners are gussied, frillier versions that come in several colors. These double flowers look like a ruffled trumpet within a trumpet. *D. metel* 'Double Blackcurrant Swirl' is a dusty lavender edged in deep purple. There is also a double-flower series called *D. metel* 'Ballerina' that comes in white, yellow, and purple.

For gardeners who have their heart set on the single white *D. metel* but cannot find it, it can sometimes be found growing as an escaped exotic. Mr. Mitchell, who was born in Memphis and later lived there as an adult for twenty years, once informed his readers that this species of devil's trumpet often grows wild on old Mississippi delta cotton plantations.

Sometimes *D. metel* is confused with *D. meteloides*, which is probably native to the American Southwest and Mexico. I say probably because daturas have been sharing their gene pool with one another for such a long time that taxonomists continue to sort out who's who. But in any case, *D. meteloides* is a single-flowered white with a growth habit similar to *D. metel*. However, the 8-inch-long and 4–6-inch-wide blossoms are tinged with the palest of lavender. I have seen this species offered in seed catalogs.

Propagate by seeds. In general, *Datura* spp. seed will germinate in 21–41 days at temperatures between 55–60 degrees. Sow indoors 6–8 weeks before last predicted frost date. Seed should be covered 1/8 inch in a well-drained potting medium. Although the plants are easy to grow, getting datura seed to germinate is not always easy for novice gardeners. USDA Hardiness Zones 6–10. AHS Heat Zones 12–6 (estimated).

Angels and Devils

There have been occasions when uninformed Yankees have called the Charleston County Clemson Extension Master Gardener office and asked where they could buy kudzu seed. I am not making this up. I was almost as incredulous when I discovered that Jimson weed *(D. stramonium)* was available for home gardens. This is the legendary plant that was mistakenly boiled for food at the Jamestown, Virginia, settlement, killing several British soldiers.

Jimsonweed leaves emit a foul smell when they are crushed. The prickly seedpods mature rapidly and split open from the top, releasing dark brown, kidney bean-shaped poisonous seeds. The 3-inch, trumpet-shaped, odoriferous flowers appear all summer long. It grows throughout the Southeast and drives peanut and cotton farmers nuts.

Plumbago

I'm a real pushover for blue flowers. Well, not all of them, and I could care less if someone eventually comes up with a blue rose. It's just that blue flowers look so handsome when they're commingled with other flower colors—especially yellow and orange—but they're also stunning by themselves. That's why I admire two blue flowering plants that are both commonly referred to as plumbago.

Ceratostigma willmottianum	**Chinese plumbago**
Plumbago auriculata	**Plumbago, cape plumbago**

Although their botanical classification places them in separate genera, *Plumbago auriculata*, commonly referred to as just plain old plumbago or sometimes leadwort, and Chinese plumbago (*Ceratostigma willmottianum*) look strikingly similar. This is because they are in the same family, *Plumbaginaceae*. Both plants display clusters of gorgeous, five-lobed, blue flowers from summer through fall. The only significant difference between the two is that *C. willmottianum* will change leaf color in the fall. Instead of staying green until frost, Chinese plumbago's diamond-shaped leaves turn red.

No matter where one places either kind in the garden (most will tolerate a little shade) these plants are guaranteed to look terrific. I must admit that I am more inclined toward *Plumbago auriculata* because I grew my first plants from seed and, therefore, have a more intimate knowledge of this plant's remarkable personality.

If a curious gardener looks up *P. auriculata* in a reference book, he or she will learn that it is native to South Africa. A standard botanical description such as "evergreen, sprawling, herbaceous shrub" will surely follow. But if I had to write such a blurb, I would definitely mention that this is a plant with a serious identity crisis.

Plumbago (*P. auriculata*) is often used as a ground cover because of its spreading habit. Over time, it will send up shoots or suckers that will eventually grow into mature shrubs. But I swear that what it really wants to be is a vine. Plant one next to a sabal palmetto that still has boots (the woody base of a frond that wraps around the trunk) and plumbago will merrily zigzag up through them. I have also seen them climbing other sturdy plants such as hollies (*Ilex* spp.).

Plumbago stems grow randomly at 45–90 degree angles at each leaf node. This feature enables them to brace themselves on wide, vertical objects that

offer corners or crevices to catch onto. The palmetto/plumbago visual effect can be stunning, although trying to get winter-burnt stems out of the boots can be a chore. Plumbago's helter-skelter stem-growth characteristic can make pruning and deadheading tedious, and I confess that I often resort to careless snipping and whacking. Gardeners who don't care to indulge in such activities can just sit back and watch *P. auriculata* grow. It will spill out into a fountain-shaped mound and will bloom all summer.

Plumbago
Plumbago auriculata

Alba Plumbago
P. auriculata

I do not recommend growing *P. auriculata* from seed. After comparing my plants to ones that were propagated from cuttings, I think that the latter makes for stronger plants. However, starting seed in late January/early February should guarantee a gardener seedlings strong enough to at least move to pots outdoors by the middle of April. Seeds will germinate at 70 degrees if they are ever so lightly covered with soil. They can take almost a month to germinate.

Plumbago is USDA Hardy to Zone 8b. Although it is considered an evergreen plant in frost-free areas, harsh winters will cause dieback. Even in Zone 8b, a hard, pipe-bursting freeze might permanently knock the life out of plumbago. However, don't be too quick to overreact. Those cinnamon-colored stems might still look dead at the end of April, but don't give up on them until as late as mid-June. Green growth from the base of the stem might start peeking through just as the plant is about to be relegated to the compost heap. For gardeners further north, I suggest making backup plants shortly before first frost. Cuttings don't mind being houseplants during the winter months and they can be planted outside after the last predicted frost date.

Plumbago now comes in various shades of blue, from a pale frosty hue to deep rich tones. 'Imperial Blue' has become a popular variety, but for those who crave a deeper blue, try Plumbago auriculata 'Monott' P. P. #7822 (Royal Cape® Plumbago). White versions are also available and one named 'Alba' is drought tolerant and slightly salt tolerant. However, it does not perform well in shade.

So which type of plumbago is best? It depends on the gardener's expectations. Both may be used for ground cover, but *P. auriculata* is taller. They are both deciduous, yet *C. willmottianum* displays colorful foliage in autumn. The following chart compares their vital statistics.

	Chinese plumbago (*Ceratostigma willmottianum*)	Plumbago (*Plumbago auriculata*)
Botanical Family	*Plumbaginaceae*	*Plumbaginaceae*
Native to	Western China and Tibet	South Africa
Habit	spreading	spreading
Use	ground cover	accent plant or ground cover
Height	1 1/2-3 feet	2-6 feet
Spread	1 1/2-3 feet	3-8 feet
Flower shape	five-lobed, slightly tubular	five-lobed, splitting into five parts
Color	blue	blue or white
Foliage	dark green, diamond shaped, turns red in fall	light green
Growth rate	moderate	fast
Flowers from	July-fall	June-fall
USDA Hardiness Zones	(6)7-9	8b-11
AHS Heat Zones	4-9	12-1
Sun	full sun to part shade	full sun to part shade
Water	medium	medium
Drought tolerance	medium	medium to high
Soil	light and loamy to poor	sterile, light and loamy, well drained
Insects and disease	minimal	minimal
Propagation	division or stem cuttings	division, stem cuttings, or seed

Portulaca
and Purslane

If you have consistently turned up your horticultural nose at the genus *Portulaca*, it's probably because these plants are sometimes not as lush as other summer-time bloomers. Yes, they can get a little leggy by the end of the season if they're not periodically pinched back, but how many other plants display lollipop-colored blossoms during a two-week August heat wave?

Portulaca grandiflora	Portulaca, moss rose
Portulaca oleracea	Purslane

Portulaca
Portulaca grandiflora

Portulaca, moss rose
Portulaca grandiflora
Annual

Portulaca (*Portulaca grandiflora*) is native to Brazil and is closely related to purslane (*P. oleracea*). Although some cultivate the latter for culinary purposes or as a desirable garden plant, many consider it a weed. Although *P. oleracea*

is probably from India, it has managed to naturalize itself in every state except Alaska. This is why one will find this plant listed in weed identification publications as well as wildflower field guides. I mention all of this because folks often inquire about that pretty little plant with the bright yellow flowers.

I too have admired *P. oleracea*. Its succulent, paddle-shaped leaves contribute to the overall attractiveness of this plant and I delight in its exceptional toughness. There is a patch of it growing at water's edge a few feet from a busy thoroughfare in downtown Charleston and nothing fazes it. It ignores road-buckling heat, drought, and monsoon rains. The only problem with this plant is that it's often overlooked because it is such a low grower. This is probably why too many people ignore its gorgeous cousin, *P. grandiflora*.

I recall hearing someone say that only small children are drawn to portulaca because they are the only ones low enough to the ground to see it. Although that's a slight exaggeration, portulaca's brilliant flower colors can't be fully appreciated unless they are seen at near eye level. Because *P. grandiflora* is as heat and drought resistant as *P. oleracea*, it too is a perfect candidate for hanging baskets and flower boxes. Get these little beauties off the ground and you'll want to start collecting every variety available.

Portulaca's growth habit is ground-hugging prostrate and rarely reaches 12 inches in height. When they're held captive in some sort of container, they will spill out over the sides, making an eye-catching statement. Most varieties stay between 4–6 inches tall with an 8–12-inch spread. The cylindrical, succulent leaves are 1 inch long.

Portulaca's flower colors come in all sorts of tantalizing "flavors." Most are so brilliant that they look like fruit-flavored hard candies. They are available in every hue but blue. Flower size will vary between 1 and 2 inches across, depending on shape and cultivar. Although all of them present a bowl-like appearance, they come in single, semi-double, or double shapes. Some of the double shapes are slightly reminiscent of roses, which sometimes confuses novice gardeners since portulaca's other common name is "moss rose."

Portulaca doesn't mind living in sandy soils. The only important growing requirement is that it receives full sun. When it is first planted, portulaca will need regular watering until it is established, but that doesn't mean it will happily spend a summer in a wet site. It is somewhat indifferent to fertilization, but leans on the less or none side.

There are so many varieties of portulaca that making choices is difficult but here is a small sample of what is available: 'Kariba Mixed' is a ruffled hybrid with cream, magenta, or red double flowers; 'Sundance' offers up semi-double red, orange, yellow, cream, and white blooms; 'Sundial Mix' is an early bloomer with double flowers that is available in apricot or peach, yellow, orange, lavender, and white.

Portulaca often self-seeds. Propagate by seed or cuttings. USDA Hardiness Zone 0–0 except in Zone 11 where it is a perennial. AHS Heat Zones 12–1.

Purslane
Portulaca oleracea
Annual and perennial

For gardeners who cannot hold on to *P. grandiflora* throughout an excessively hot *and* exceptionally humid summer, there are spruced up and terribly proper cultivars of *P. oleracea* (aka purslane) that are as handsome as they are tough. Although there are now double forms such as 'Summer Joy Scarlet,' 'Sleeping Beauty,' 'Snow White,' and 'Cinderella,' I'm still smitten with the Yubi series' single form. My favorite, 'Yubi Scarlet,' is a real showstopper. The color is a glowing neon pinkish orange with a bright yellow center. For gardeners who prefer a softer effect, 'Yubi Light Pink' is very dainty while 'Yubi Rose' is quite regal.

Propagate by seed or cuttings. USDA Hardiness Zone 0–0 except in Zone 11 where it is a perennial. AHS Heat Zones 12–1.

Portulaca
Portulaca grandiflora

Zinnias

I wonder how many people began their lifelong love of gardening when, as kids, an adult handed them a pack of zinnia seeds and showed them how to sow them. I still get a kick out of seeing zinnias' vibrant colors at the height of summer, so I'm always puzzled when someone apologizes for growing them.

Zinnia spp.
Z. augustifolia
Z. elegans
Annual

"Oh, they're only zinnias," they'll say, or joke about growing such a common plant. Well, maybe zinnias are common in the sense that their ancestors were weedy, little, reddish purple flowers with daisy-like petals. They grew wild in what was old Mexico and parts of Central America.

Zinnia
Z. augustifolia

Like folks in other regions, Deep South gardeners took to growing zinnias in the early 1880s, probably on the advice of the ever-so-correct Victorian gardening publication, *Vick's Monthly Magazine*. Zinnias were to be cultivated at the edge of the backyard where they could be admired from a window. It seems funny that we now grow them everywhere imaginable yet feign horticultural embarrassment for doing it.

I will be the first to admit that some zinnias can be tough to grow in hot and humid weather. After losing the battle against the fungus called powdery mildew several summers ago, I vowed never to grow them again. However, with the introduction of more disease resistant varieties, they are making a comeback in southeastern summer gardens.

Before we go any farther, a few words about powdery mildew are in order. It's a sure sign of summer when concerned gardeners begin calling the Charleston County Extension Service Master Gardener office in late May or early June with concerns about powdery mildew on crepe myrtles (*Lagerstroemia* spp.). One of their first questions is, "Will it infect my other plants?" The whitish gray stuff that coats crepe myrtle leaves is named *Erysiphe lagerstroemia*, and it is specific only to *Lagerstroemia* spp. Other powdery mildews behave similarly. For example, the disease that harms roses is called *Sphaerotheca pannosa*, but this kind of powdery mildew will only harm roses.

The powdery mildew that is notorious for ravishing zinnias is named *Erysiphe cichoracearum*. It specifically targets plants in the Composit family that, unfortunately, also includes dahlias, sunflowers, and chrysanthemums. Does this mean that Deep South gardeners are doomed never to grow any of these plants? Of course not. There are two ways to get around this problem.

First, good cultural practices are a must and they are not that difficult to perform. Susceptible plants should be grown in as much sun as possible because powdery mildew thrives in cool, shady, moist spots. Good air circulation is also a must. Yes, a tightly mixed color medley of zinnias looks spectacular, but please give them enough room to breath. Furthermore, skip the high-octane fertilizer. A slow-release fertilizer deprives powdery mildew of those big energy boosts that it craves. And for all the gardeners who love to play with the garden hose, here is your big opportunity. When powdery mildew spores land in water they croak, so spraying zinnias with abandon will flush off the bad guys. The best time for this entertainment is in the morning. Allowing plants the chance to thoroughly dry off before the evening dews return will help to prevent other disease problems. Prolonged wetness is a guaranteed prescription for all sorts of ills.

The second way to avoid powdery mildew is to plant disease-resistant plants. Single-blossom hybrids such as 'Pinwheel' and 'Profusion' are tough plants that live up to their disease-free promise. 'Pinwheel' has been available for many years. Their 3-inch blooms hold their color for several days before

fading, but deadheading will perk up the flowering pace in no time. Colors come in light pink to dark rose, pale orange to deeper hues, and white. All have a yellowish eye. These 1-foot-tall plants look best when grown in a mass. My only disappointment in these plants has been with how their seeds are marketed. I have only seen 'Pinwheel' sold in packets of mixed colors, so if a specific one is desired, one is out of luck.

On the other hand, 'Profusion' seeds are available in single colors, which include cherry, orange, and white. They too have yellow eyes. These All-American Winners are quite bushy and will spread to 2 feet. They are slightly taller than the 'Pinwheel' series and will reach 1 1/2-feet.

The narrow-leafed zinnias (*Zinnia augustifolia*), which are also tough against powdery mildew, have a growth habit that makes them excellent candidates for ground covers. They also make attractive edgings along large beds because their height remains at 8–12 inches. Colors range from white through yellow and orange. The 'Star' series, as well as the 'Crystal' series, are low-maintenance plants. But if they start to get out of hand or begin to look scraggly, these zinnias can easily be cut back into shape without worrying about correct pruning practices.

When anyone mentions zinnias, the ones with dahlia-shaped blossoms probably come first to mind. These plants

Zinnia
Zinnia elegans

are botanically named *Zinnia elegans* and they are available in a mind-boggling bounty of varieties. My favorite selection is from the 'Dreamland' series. These 2-feet-tall sweeties can sometimes drive southeastern gardeners nuts with powdery mildew, but in some years, the problem is so negligible that it's hardly noticeable.

Sowing more seed in the bed after the first batch is up and growing is one way some gardeners keep their 'Dreamland' zinnias looking fresh all summer, even when powdery mildew encroaches. If some plants must be removed because of disease, younger backup plants are ready to step in.

I could have put zinnias in the *in situ* section because their seed is often sown outdoors after the last predicted freeze date and, of course, that's perfectly acceptable. However, because some zinnias grown in the Deep South can be vulnerable to powdery mildew, I think it best to start them indoors 4–6 weeks before the last frost and then thoughtfully space them out when transplanting outdoors. You'll need bottom heat to get them to germinate indoors and, since zinnias often resent transplanting, they should be started in individual peat pots. But the extra effort is worth it because it allows the planter the opportunity to make sure that the zinnias will have enough breathing room at maturity. It is just too tempting to leave most if not all *in situ* grown seedlings in the ground instead of thinning them out when they are babies. This leads to overcrowding, which is a surefire way to tempt disease. When soil temperatures reach 70–80 degrees, seed may be lightly scattered in the beds and covered with 1/16-inch of soil. Expect germination in about 10–24 days. And don't forget to thin if you planted too much seed.

'Dreamland' zinnias are shorter and more compact than some of the old-fashioned, 4-foot-tall varieties. They will stay about 1 foot tall. Their mounding growth habit can spread from 8–36 inches. 'Dreamland' zinnias send out 4-inch-diameter double flowers that come in apricot, creamy white, red, pink, yellow, and orange. One color, 'Scarlet Splendor,' was an All-American winner in 1990.

All *Z. elegans* need to be deadheaded and 'Dreamland' is no exception. They make splendid cut flowers. For gardeners who are interested in other kinds of *Z. elegans*, I highly recommend perusing Allan Armitage's extensive photographs of zinnias in his *Armitage's Garden Annuals: A Color Encyclopedia*.

Propagate by seed. USDA Hardiness Zones 0–0. AHS Heat Zones 12–1.

Plants with Interesting Foliage or Leaf Color

When we dream about the ideal summer garden for the hot and sultry Deep South, most of us probably think of annual and perennial flowers first. A riot of continuous bloom insinuates that whoever is doing the gardening certainly knows their stuff.

H owever, try to imagine a setting without trees or shrubs. Without these plants we'd be stuck with acres of colorful, prairie-looking gardens and nothing else.

Trees and shrubs are the anchors that give our gardens their individual, often unique, identities by adding depth and texture. Some larger herbaceous perennials can do that too. But instead of being admired for their flowers, these plants display leaf shapes or colors that can bring excitement to well-thought-out yet boring garden designs.

This special group of plants offers gentle transitions from woody to herbaceous settings. Many can also be used as ground covers and all make great accents when grown as specimens. Several add height and balance to container plantings and all offer themselves as foils to other smaller, showier plants.

My selection is hardly an inclusive list for southeastern gardens. Some of my choices may be terribly familiar to experienced gardeners, but they are tried and true friends who continue to deserve our admiration. I have also included two plants that, botanically speaking, are not herbaceous perennials. Although cycads are considered shrubs, they can look fabulous in herbaceous borders and, as a consequence, are worthy of mention.

At the end of the next chapter are at-a-glance lists that categorize specific characteristics of these special plants.

Cycads
Cardboard palm
Zamia furfuracea
Florida arrowroot
Zamia intergrifolia
Perennial

If you have ever tried to find gardening information about sago palms (*Cycas circinalis*) in a book about palm trees, then you probably ended up completely confused or at least nonplussed. Isn't a sago palm a palm tree? This is a clas-

Sago palm
Cycas circinalis

sic example of what happens when we rely on common names instead of botanical ones. And don't be embarrassed if you fell into the if-it-looks-like-a palm-and-acts-like-a-palm snare. Sagos may have palm-shaped fronds and skinny, scruffy trunks just like palm trees, but these plants are not even closely related. In fact, sagos, along with the rest of their Cycad relatives, are botanically allied to pine trees (*Pinus* spp.) and gingkoes (*Gingko biloba*). They are all coniferous plants. Instead of containing seed in an ovary, conifer seed is arranged helically on an external, spore-bearing leaf called a sporophyll. The orange fruit that grows in the center of a sago palm is actually a cone and its shape identifies the sex of the plant.

Although I like sago palms as much as anyone else, they've become terribly overused in the landscape. To reinforce my point about excessiveness, I recently counted sago palms along a less than half-mile route on peninsular Charleston. I stopped counting after the twelfth one. Our monomaniacal focus on just one kind of Cycad is unfortunate. Two hundred eighty-nine species belong to the ancient order of Cycadales. While only five genera contain species that are cultivated for horticultural purposes, we appear to be enjoying only one of them.

Two Zamias deserve consideration for hot and humid gardens. Both are somewhat fernlike in appearance and would make fine substitutes in situations where ferns might not grow. My favorite also has a confusing common name. It's called the cardboard palm (*Zamia furfuracea*).

Cardboard palm
Zamia furfuracea

Cardboard palm
Zamia furfuracea

Cardboard palm
Zamia furfuracea
Small evergreen shrub

Cycads have been around for more than 200 million years and were a food source for dinosaurs. Although I have never read that prehistoric herbivores relished cardboard palms, these plants certainly look like brontosaurus snacks. *Zamia furfuracea's* stems branch out from an underground main trunk to form a crown of stiff evergreen leaves. Each leaf contains ten to forty rather thick, pale green, very oblong, 6–7-inch-long leaflets that are 1–2 1/2 inches wide. They look so ridged and crowded together that one expects them to clatter against one another in the wind. Yes, they look a little like cardboard and the lack of visible leaf veins adds to their artificial appearance. If prehistoric animals consumed this plant, they must have done so very carefully. Cardboard fern's petioles are accoutered with very sharp spines.

Loran M. Whitelock, author of *The Cycads*, says that cardboard palms rate right behind sagos in popularity, yet I only know of one growing in Charleston (USDA Hardiness Zone 8b). It's a specimen plant that's happily thriving at Trident Technical College's arboretum. I have been told that retail garden centers are sometimes reluctant to carry cardboard palms because, when these fern-like plants are young and growing in 1- to 3-gallon containers, they tend to look downright ugly. They often sport only two or three very unsymmetrical "fronds" at this tender stage, so gardeners are inclined to scoff, then wander off to find more attractive landscape material.

Those who are willing to take a chance on such funny-looking youngsters will certainly be rewarded. In addition to being real showstoppers, cardboard palms are fairly nonchalant about their growing conditions as long as they are kept out of places with poor drainage. They are indifferent to soil types, require average amounts of water, and are drought tolerant. This small shrub (2–5 feet) has an overall roundish growth habit with a spread of 5–8 feet. It will grow in sun or part shade.

Botanists have been known to rave about this plant's ability to adapt to almost any kind of environmental conditions. Although *Z. furfuracea* thrives in hot and humid weather, it also flourishes in arid Mediterranean regions. Cardboard palms make excellent beach plants because they are salt tolerant, will grow in almost pure sand, and are happy in scorching full sun. In fact, the more sun they receive, the more compact their growth habit.

These glowing testimonials come with a caveat. If temperatures fall below 27 degrees for an extended period, cardboard palms may not pull through the winter. This means that gardeners north of USDA Hardiness Zone 9b must figure out a way to protect cardboard palms in winter. Mulching helps and making sure the main trunk is completely planted below the ground adds some extra insurance. Then again, there's always the southern approach to cold weather gardening. Dig it out, put in a pot, and haul it off to the garage.

Cardboard palms can be propagated by division or seed. USDA Hardiness Zones (8)9–11. AHS Heat Zones 12–7 (estimated).

Florida arrowroot
Zamia intergrifolia
Small evergreen shrub
Although Florida arrowroot (*Zamia intergrifolia*) may be native to Florida, it has a South Carolina connection. In 1767, Charleston's very own Scottish Tory,

Dr. Alexander Garden, the man for whom the gardenia was named, sent some Florida arrowroot plants back to England. His description of them was quite apt. He suggested to his colleagues to think of a fern with a *magnolia grandiflora* cone—berries and all—growing from the center.

Botanists have been arguing about Florida arrowroot's taxonomy once Carl Linnaeus's son finally got around to writing about this plant some twenty years after Dr. Garden's account. Although the botanical debate is of little interest to home gardeners, it is worth noting that arrowroot's scientific name may vary depending upon which side you take. I mention this only because you might meet someone who thinks this plant should be called *Z. floridana* or *Z. angustifolia* or *Z. silvicola* or *Z. umbrosa*. I have read that it is also common for some to confuse it with *Z. pumila*. Perhaps the best way to avoid an argument is to call it Florida zamia and leave it at that. But then again, *Z. floridana* and *Z. pumila* are also native to Florida, so you're still taking chances.

The plant's common name is derived from its original purpose. The Seminole Indians processed the stems to make a thickener that was used in cooking. Hence the name "Florida arrowroot." It looks very similar to its cardboard palm cousin except that its leaflets are slightly thinner and longer. The leaf stems grow in a slightly twisted fashion, which accentuates its movement when the wind blows. Its main trunk is subterranean and the evergreen leaves emerge in a crownlike fashion. It makes a nice accent plant or take advantage of its 1 1/2–2 1/2-foot height and 3-foot spread to make an interesting ground cover.

Some southern gardeners may already be familiar with this plant. The Florida highway department has used native zamias for landscaping along freeways. That's certainly an excellent testimonial to its toughness. Florida arrowroot will thrive in dunes, savannahs, piney woods, and deciduous forests. It will grow in sun or partial shade.

USDA Hardiness Zones 8–11. AHS Heat Zones 12–7 (estimated).

Cycads

If pampas grass (*Cortaderia selloana*) takes the Twins-at-the-End-of-the-Driveway Award, then the sago palm wins the same at the front of the house. Why are we so committed to having identical plants on both sides of our front doors or gates? (Try breaking up the symmetry by planting two on one side and only one on the other.) I also wonder if these oh-so-symmetrical home-owners know exactly what kind of *Cycas* they have planted.

The problem is that *C. circinalis* and *C. revoluta* are both called sago palm. When they are young and growing low to the ground, it's easy to confuse them. However, *C. circinalis* will eventually put out 8-foot-long "fronds" and its trunk can reach twenty feet in height. This is the plant that looks like a palm tree. Although *C. revoluta's* main stem is sometimes seen above ground on mature plants, this species will never get tall enough to look like a palm tree. The best it can ever do is reach about half the height of its cousin.

C. revoluta is a slow grower that usually stays between 3–5 feet tall and 4–8 feet wide. However, it is often planted too close to a structure when purchased in a small, gallon-sized container. Gardeners should remember to give them enough space for their eventual mature size. Bumping into these very stiff, frondlike leaves can be unpleasant. Many quickly learn to take an alternate route to avoid another confrontation.

Although both kinds of *Cycas* can be grown from seed, *C. revoluta* will sometimes produce suckers at the base of the trunk. These pups, as they're called, can be gently severed from the mother plant and potted up.

Horticulturally speaking, *C. circinalis* and *C. revoluta* are considered evergreen shrubs with a palm plant habit. If you can't find information about them in a shrub listing, switch to the palms category and you'll more than likely find them there. However, expect to read a disclaimer about them not really being palms. Go figure.

Purple Heart
Setcreasea pallida

Purple Heart, Purple Queen
Setcreasea pallida (Setcreasea purpurea)
Annual or perennial

Purple heart (*Setcreasea pallida*) is found in some of the darnedest places in Charleston. This ubiquitous, dark purple plant grows freely along edges of alleys and side streets and thrives in abandoned flowerbeds. Some folks pamper purple heart in extravagant containers while others simply stick it in whatever is handy. It is one of the most overused and underappreciated plants in the Deep South and I didn't care one whit about it until I grew one on a windowsill.

Years ago, a friend had insisted that this plant was commonly known as Moses in a boat (*Rhoeo spathacea*). I thought it had a name like purple-passion-something. It turns out that we were arguing about two different plants but both are in the spiderwort family. They share similar characteristics, including charming but almost inconspicuous flowers that are snugged inside two bracts above each leaf base. But it wasn't until the College of Charleston began planting copious amounts of purple heart in huge outdoor pots that I felt compelled to correctly identify this plant. With pruners in hand, I strolled out for a cutting.

After I returned home and placed a 4-inch stem with a couple of lanceolate leaves in a vase, I became nonplussed about my acquisition's true identity. One source said my cutting was a *S. pallida* while another listed it as *S. purpurea.* Further poking around led me to discover that, although purple heart's botanical name had been changed to *S. pallida* ages ago, many continue to use the former one.

My cutting was also missing one of purple heart's defining characteristics—hairy, white leaf fuzz. Several months later, my example began to display this distinguishing trait. It's very subtle and doesn't pick up in the light unless the angle is just so. I have since noticed that this attribute is difficult to find on plants that are grown outdoors.

Purple heart's three-petaled flowers with twice as many stamens are the dead giveaway that it is a spiderwort. Its pale pink to light lavender blossoms with sunny yellow stamens are attractive but, unless one is close up and at eye level, the flowers often go unnoticed. Instead, purple heart is grown for its leaf and stem color as well as its habit. Some use it as a ground cover while others prefer to let it scramble down hanging baskets and flowerpots. Although not a vine, purple heart's long, succulent stems and 4–6-inch, lance-shaped leaves often behave like one. Its dark color makes a fabulous foil against true vines such as the outrageously overused, lime green sweet potato vine (*Ipomoea batatas* 'Chartreuse'). For a more dramatic effect, let purple heart snuggle up to the cream, green, and pink leaved *I. batatas* 'Tricolor.'

Tricolor sweet potato vine
I. batatas 'Tricolor'

Although purple heart is usually considered a passalong plant, varieties are available. *S. pallida* 'Variegata' is purple and pink (USDA Hardiness Zones (7–10) and 'Kartuz Giant' (*S. pallida* 'Kartuz Giant') is about three times the size of the straight species (USDA Hardiness Zones 7b–10). This brute's 2-feet clumps and slightly curled leaf tips make an impressive statement in a border or large container.

One might assume that the blazing sun would surely scorch a deep purple plant, but *S. pallida* grows in sun or shade. This Mexican amigo can take walloping doses of heat, plus humidity, and never flinch. It's also a great plant for the seashore because it tolerates salt. Its immunity to drought makes it a good ground cover, especially under trees. Its maximum height is between 1–1 1/2 feet. A moderate grower, its spread is indeterminate, but spacing purple heart at 1-foot intervals should insure quick coverage. Do remember to keep it well watered until it becomes established. Even drought-tolerant plants need moisture while settling in.

Purple heart is not particular about soil as long as it is moist and well drained. It is a perennial in USDA Hardiness Zones 8–11. If leaves and stems

Spiderwort

Those three-petaled, bright blue flowers with the yellow stamens that sprout up in abundance during a southeastern spring are called spiderworts (*Tradescantia virginiana*). These native plants are related to *S. pallida* and both belong to the spiderwort family (*Commelinaceae*).

About twenty different kinds of spiderworts are scattered throughout North and South America and all are easy to identify because every clue has to do with threes. They all have three petals, three sepals (which makes up the bractlike calyx), and six stamens. Flower colors range from white, pink, red, blue, and purple.

are frozen in winter, they usually come back from the roots in spring. Prune it down to the ground after first frost. Purple heart is mostly disease and pest free.

Propagate by cuttings at any time. USDA Hardiness Zones (7)8–11 (grown as an annual in others). AHS Heat Zones 12–1.

Persian Shield
Strobilanthes dyerianus
Annual and perennial

My colored leaf threshold must be pretty high. I have become so accustomed to seeing masses of cream and pink caladiums (*Caladium bicolor*) planted under Charleston's live oaks that I no longer notice them. Ditto for coleus (*Coleus* x *hybridus*), except when they're allowed to bolt, looking even more ridiculous than before. I was, therefore, quite surprised when I caught myself ogling a small bed of Persian shield (*Strobilanthes dyerianus*) at our local technical school's arboretum. It was a windy afternoon and Persian shield's metallic purple leaves almost glistened under an overcast sky.

Persian shield is native to Burma, so it goes without saying that it likes hot and humid weather. In fact, its growth rate increases when summer days turn miserable for the rest of us. Depending on which USDA Hardiness Zone it is in, Persian shield can be grown as an annual or perennial. In Zone 9b and further south, it can mature into a small, sturdy shrub about 3–5 feet tall with a 3-foot spread. The rest of us will have to accept a slightly shorter 24–30-inch-tall plant. But no matter where it is grown, Persian shield's mature 6-inch leaves are real showstoppers. The slightly oval, usually lanceolate leaves are solid dark magenta on the bottom while the upper part looks rather like a medieval church window. The veins are dark and appear to be holding pieces of shiny purple glass between them. As the leaves mature, the purple softens to pink. The overall effect is sensational.

Persian shield is grown for its appealing foliage and not its flowers. Although one would think that pale blue blossoms against such majestic col-

Persian Shield
Strobilanthes
dyerianusida

ors would look smashing, they don't add one whit to *S. dyerianus'* overall beauty. Chances are that few of us will ever see them bloom in our gardens, but when Persian shield blooms for nurserymen, they cringe.

For some odd reason, and no one has quite figured it out, *S. dyerianus* cuttings do not propagate well once they have started to flower. It's as if the process of reproduction shuts down Persian shield. Even when propagation is successful, new plants usually don't make it to the marketplace because they aren't as healthy or vibrant as the mother plants. It has also been observed that an otherwise strapping *S. dyerianus* never regains its vegetative vigor after blooming. Because Persian shield's reproductive cycle begins in early winter, some theorize that shorter daylight length (photoperiodism), cooler temperatures, or both, might be the cause of this anomaly.

Persian shield can take sun but will not sulk in shade. Although leaf color coincides with light intensity, planting it where it will receive continuous blazing hot afternoon sun is probably not wise. This plant's tropical heritage means that it needs plenty of moisture in a well-drained situation. Giving it plenty of organic material will trap water

like a sponge without keeping roots too soggy. Persian shield is not drought or salt tolerant and can sometimes be susceptible to whitefly.

Propagate by cuttings. USDA Hardiness Zones 8–11. AHS Heat Zones unknown.

Victorian Friends in Modern Gardens

What is it about ferns and Victorian-style houses? Why do so many of us associate the two together? I accidentally stumbled upon a reasonable answer several years ago and I still like it.

Aspidistra elatior	**Cast Iron Plant**
Cyrtomium falcatum	**Holly Fern**
(C. imbricatum)	
Osmunda cinnamomea	**Cinnamon Fern**
Thelypteris kunthii	**Southern Shield Fern,**
	Widespread Maiden Fern

Landscape expert William Robinson (1838–1935) was a Victorian gardener who fervently believed that ferns were an important addition to any respectable garden. This Irishman-turned-Londoner is credited with creating the late-1800s fern craze in Great Britain, which was then repeated in the U.S.

Cast iron plant (*Aspidistra elatior*) was also admired and cultivated during the Victorian era. Many photographs of parlors include an obligatory potted aspidistra standing at attention on a pedestal in a corner.

Southern gardeners are lucky because we have never had to relegate our ferns and cast iron plants to indoor cultivation only. Our climate is usually warm enough to keep many of these plants in our gardens throughout the year. These utilitarian friends can be treated as accent plants or used as ground covers. They add height and texture to any herbaceous border and create smooth transitions from taller, woody ornamentals to lower-growing flowering annuals and perennials.

Cast Iron Plant
Aspidistra elatior
Evergreen perennial
Aspidistra elatior is sometimes called barroom plant because it shrugs off adversities such as low light, poor air quality, and neglect. In other words, aspidistra is as tough as cast iron. Northerners grow it as a houseplant and florists frequently use its slender, lance-shaped leaves as accents in arrangements. Southern gardeners turn it loose as a ground cover or use it as an accessory in herbaceous borders. Unfortunately, too many of us expect the cast iron plant to do more than it is capable of.

Aspidistra doesn't ask for much, but it cannot take too much sun. Hit it with all the heat and humidity a southeastern summer can muster and it will

Cast Iron Plant
Aspidistra elatior

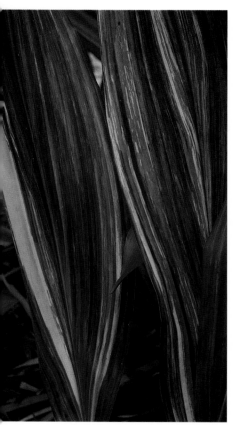

Cast Iron Plant 'Variegata'
A. elatior

continue to cheerfully push up new single leaves from the soil while remaining relatively insect free and disease resistant. But give it one speck too much sunlight and its leaves will turn a sickly yellow.

Aspidistra rebels if it receives full sun. However, if it is given generous amounts of shade, it will reward you with shiny, lance-like, 2 1/2-feet tall and 3–4-inch-wide dark green leaves all year long. Come on, y'all. Did you think a plant that survives in dim indoor light should be expected to take intense outdoor sunlight—especially in the Deep South? I have seen so many inappropriate planting schemes around Charleston that I'm about to start an Aspidistra Rescue Society.

One of the things that I love about aspidistra is that it's not intrusive. Yes, it will spread at a moderate rate but it seems to be incapable of completely overstepping its bounds. It slowly spreads by tough, thick rhizomes. We had to remove a 2 x 5-foot swath one summer and, much to my embarrassment, I couldn't get the aspidistra out of the ground. After our mason graciously dug it out (he struggled too), I placed the evicted plants on top of a shaded compost heap. Although they sat there for two weeks and I kept forgetting to water them, they all survived.

Most southern gardeners are familiar with the standard, glossy green, single-leaved version of cast iron plant. However, *A. elatior* 'Variegata' sports subtle, creamy white vertical stripes. Although a large bed of striped ones might look as silly as a Spike Jones jacket, a few peeking out among a gathering of straight species adds interest to an otherwise monotonous sea of green. However, even the slightest amount of sun will cause the streaks to temporarily disappear. Although the leaves will remain dark green, 'Variegata' needs plenty of shade to show off its vertical streaks.

For gardeners not interested in stripes but who still prefer a showier aspidistra, *A. elatior* 'Milky Way' is rather like a Jackson Pollack creation because it is flecked with yellow spots. This variety also comes in a dwarf form (cleverly named *A. elatior* 'Dwarf Milky Way') and performs well in deep shade. Another cultivar, *A. elatior* 'Asahi,' is sometimes called frosted cast iron plant. This is because the tips are lighter green than the rest of the leaf. Although it can take deep shade, giving it dappled sunlight and small doses of low nitrogen fertilizer will encourage the frosted effect.

Aspidistra prefers moist soils that are high in organic material, but it will grow in sandy soils and will tolerate moderate bouts of drought. This plant is relatively maintenance free, but when a leaf begins to die, or displays shredded or tattered tips, cut the thick-as-a-soda-straw stem at ground level with pruners. Aspidistra is relatively insect free, but scale can occasionally be an annoyance— more to the gardener than the plant. I have, on occasion, sprayed in the spring with a dormant oil spray in an attempt to thwart these pests, but have decided that pruning out a few infected leaves is just as effective. Since aspidistra seems to enjoy periodic sprucings and light thinnings, this chore has multiple benefits. It looks healthier and happier and sends out new growth.

Propagate by digging up and dividing clumps. USDA Hardiness Zones 7–11. AHS Heat Zone unknown.

Holly Fern

Cyrtomium falcatum (*C. imbricatum*)

Evergreen perennial

I have been with novice gardeners who stop and admire leatherleaf mahonia (*Mahonia bealei*) with the exclamation that they just love holly ferns (*Cyrtomium falcatum*). Obviously, this is not when leatherleaf mahonia is displaying its fabulous robins-egg blue drupes. True, both plants have slightly similar looking, alternate, glossy green, hollylike leaflets. However, leatherleaf mahonia's are clustered at the stem tip and holly fern's are not. But the easiest way to distinguish the two is to look under the leaves. Fern fronds display spore cases on the back of their leaflets.

Holly Fern
Cyrtomium falcatum

Cinnamon Fern
Osmunda cinnamomea

Holly fern is native to parts of the South Pacific and southern Asia, so it feels at home with our hot and humid summers. If protected from excessive cold, its glossy green leaves will add holiday cheer to a winter garden. They prefer to be planted away from summer sun and cruel northern and western winter winds. They also like to be snuggled up next to trees or shrubs for additional summer shade and winter protection. Their mature height is between 24–30 inches, with fronds spreading out to 30 inches. Planting holly fern about 1 1/2 feet from a bigger plant or structure will be appreciated.

Too much sun or cold will turn holly fern leaflets to a pathetic yellow, with crispy brown burns along the edges. If this occurs during the winter, it's best to leave these unsightly fronds untouched until spring. Although they look unattractive, they offer the rest of the plant some protection from the cold. Removing them makes the fern more vulnerable to harsh elements. If holly ferns look dead and scorched at winter's end, be patient. New growth may start to appear once warmer temperatures return. That is when the unsightly old growth can be removed. Follow the frond stem back to the center of the clump and cut with sharp pruners. Unattractive fronds may be removed throughout the summer.

Holly ferns prefer fertile, loamy soils that are continually moist; not damp or soggy, but never dry. They also enjoy the same special fertilizer that is used on azaleas, camellias, and other acid-loving plants.

Propagate by rhizome division in spring. USDA Hardiness Zones 6–10. AHS Heat Zones 12–7.

Cinnamon Fern
Osmunda cinnamomea
Deciduous perennial

Those ferns that Southerners admire growing wild around the edges of swamps and wetlands are probably cinnamon ferns (*Osmunda cinnamomea*). They are native to the southeast and, although they are inclined to prefer silt or clay soils, can make respectable garden accents in most any kind of soil as long as they get plenty of water. Gardeners with troublesome wet spots should consider planting cinnamon ferns there. Although they prefer shade, partial sun will do them no harm as long as there is ample moisture.

Cinnamon ferns will reach a height of about 3–5 feet with a 2–3-foot width. Their showy green fronds will mature to 8-inches wide and will turn bronze in the fall. Their fuzzy, rusty colored fiddleheads add interest and color to a springtime garden. Cinnamon ferns are sometimes slow growers when they are first planted. However, once they are established, they will live for many years.

Propagate by dividing rhizomes in late winter. USDA Hardiness Zones 2–10. AHS Heat Zones 9–1.

Southern Shield Fern, Widespread Maiden Fern
Thelypteris kunthii
Deciduous perennial

When we were living in Virginia, a friend gave us a large, healthy Boston fern (*Nephrolepis exaltata*). Houseplant enthusiasts usually covet such plants and I was honored to be the recipient of such an attractive fern. We kept it outside until it got too cold and that's when the trouble began. To me, it smelled unpleasantly musty and I found myself not liking to be around it. As a result, it didn't get watered very often and I was actually relieved when it died. Then, after we moved to Charleston, I grew weary of listening to well-meaning Yankees insist that we hang baskets of you-know-what from our piazza. Must

Southern Shield Fern,
Widespread Maiden Fern
Thelypteris kunthii

ferns always be obligatory accessories for Victorian houses? Well, not ours, thank you.

That was until 1989 and Hurricane Hugo left behind a gazillion spores in the scraggly border at the bottom of the piazza. When I first discovered a few tiny ferns popping up that following spring, I was nonplussed and left them there, convinced that they'd never make it through a long hot summer in a southwestern exposure. By the time summer was about to end, passersby kept wanting to know how I had managed to grow such spectacular plants in such a short time after a hurricane.

Like the cinnamon fern, southern shield fern is native to the Southeast and needs plenty of moisture if grown in the sun. The soft, lime green leaves can withstand drought if planted in the shade, but once deprived of water in hot sunshine will turn a purplish bronze before shriveling to a crisp brown. It is not particular about soil type as long as it is continuously moist. Southern shield fern fronds can grow 2–4 feet tall. At the widest part, frond length is sometimes as much as 10 inches. Frond clusters usually range from 4–7 or 8 per bunch, so the widths can vary from 12 inches up to 3–4 feet. This fern spreads by shallow underground rhizomes. When clumps get too large they can easily be removed with a garden hoe, or sometimes by hand if the soil is moist.

Southern shield ferns are deciduous and their leaflets will shrivel and turn brown after first frost. Foliage should not be cut down until after the last projected freeze date the following spring. The spent fronds will protect the rhizomes from cold damage and, if other herbaceous plants are commingled with them, they too will benefit from the southern shield fern's protection.

Although I'm crazy about southern shield fern because when used as a ground cover its additional height complements taller structures, I don't like to work in or around it. It has that same reminiscent musty odor as Boston fern. I mention this only as a warning to those who might share my displeasure.

I have found that removing old fronds is easier and faster if hedge clippers are used instead of cutting each frond with pruners. I have also used electric hedge shears when large swaths need to be cleared. Cut back dead growth to the ground in early spring and don't worry about accidental fiddlehead loss. Wearing boots or sturdy shoes, long pants and gardening gloves is highly recommended. Frond stubble is tough and can leave splinters in fingers. After clean up, apply mulch before new growth begins to appear.

Propagate by division. USDA Hardiness Zones 7–11. AHS Heat Zones 12–7 (estimated).

Plants with Interesting Foliage Guide

Nothing takes the chill out of a winter's day like planning a garden. But by the time I'm ready to head out to the garden centers or place some catalog orders, I've often accumulated so many notes about the plants I want that it's difficult to keep everything straight. Because plants that are cultivated for their foliage are often used as backgrounds for smaller flowering ones, their placement in the garden should be considered first. Think of it this way: No one purchases accessories and then tries to find an outfit to match.

Plants with Interesting Foliage That Prefer Full Sun or Partial Shade

Botanical Name	Common Name	Attributes	Height	Spread	Soil Requirements	Drought Tolerance	USDA Hardiness Zones	AHS Heat Zones	Annual or Perennial
Strobilanthes dyerianus	Persian shield	Purple leaves	3–5 ft.	3 ft.	Well-drained, moist and loamy	None	9–11	Unknown	P
Strobilanthes dyerianus	Persian shield	Purple leaves	24–30 in.	3 ft.	Well-drained, moist and loamy	None, sandy	8	Unknown	A
Thelypteris kunthii	Southern shield fern	Soft, lime green fronds	2–4 ft.	1–4 ft.	Any type as long as it's moist	Low	7–11	9–1 (est.)	P
Zamia intergrifolia	Florida arrowroot	Interesting leaf shape	1 1/2–2 1/2 ft.	3 ft.	Indifferent	High	8–11	12–7 (est.)	P

Plants with Interesting Foliage That Prefer Shade

Botanical Name	Common Name	Attributes	Height	Spread	Soil Requirements	Drought Tolerance	USDA Hardiness Zones	AHS Heat Zones	Annual or Perennial
Aspidistra elatior	Cast iron plant	Evergreen. Dark green leaf shape	2 1/2 ft.	2–3 ft. clumps	Loamy to sandy	Moderate	7–11	Unknown	P
Aspidistra elatior 'Asahi'	Cast iron plant	Evergreen. Lighter green on tips or frosted effect	2 1/2 ft.	2–3 ft. clumps	Loamy to sandy	Moderate	7–11	Unknown	P
Aspidistra elatior '*Dwarf Milky Way*'	Cast iron plant	Evergreen. Flecked with yellow spots	1 1/2 ft.	1 1/2– 2 ft. clumps	Loamy to sandy	Moderate	7–11	Unknown	P
Aspidistra elatior '*Variegata*'	Cast iron plant	Evergreen. Creamy white vertical stripes	2 1/2 ft.	2–3 ft. clumps	Loamy to sandy	Moderate	7–11	Unknown	P
Aspidistra a elatior 'Milky Way'	Cast iron plant	Evergreen. Flecked with yellow spots	2 1/2 ft.	2–3 ft. clumps	Loamy to sandy	Moderate	7–11	Unknown	P

Plants With Interesting Foliage That Prefer Shade and Filtered Sun

Botanical Name	Common Name	Attributes	Height	Spread	Soil Requirement	Drought Tolerance	USDA Hardiness Zones	AHS Heat Zones	Annual or Perennial
Cyrtomium falcatum (C. imbricatum)	Holly fern	Evergreen. Shiny, dark green, hollylike leaves	24–30 in.	30 in.	Moist and loamy	Low	6–10	12–7	P
Osmunda cinnamomea	Cinnamon fern	Deciduous. Fuzzy, cinnamon colored fiddle-heads. Bronze fronds in fall	3–5 ft.	2–3 ft.	Any type as long as it's moist	Low	2–10	9–1	P

Plants With Interesting Foliage That Will Grow in Sun or Shade

Botanical Name	Common Name	Attributes	Height	Spread	Soil Requirement	Drought Tolerance	USDA Hardiness Zones	AHS Heat Zones	Annual or Perennial
Setcreasea pallida	Purple heart	Purple leaves	1–1 1/2 ft.	Indeterminate	Moist and well-drained	High	(7)8–11	12–1	P
Setcreasea pallida 'Kartzu Giant'	'Kartzu Giant' purple heart	Purple leaves	2-1/2–3 ft.	2-foot clumps	Moist and well-drained	High	7b–10	12–1	P
Setcreasea pallida 'Variegata'	Variegated purple heart	Pink and purple leaves	1–1 1/2 ft.	Indeterminate	Moist and well-drained	High	7–10	12–1	P
Zamia furfuracea	Cardboard palm	Interesting leaf shape	2–5 ft.	5–8 ft.	Indifferent	High	(8)9–11	12–7 (est.)	P

Plants With Interesting Foliage That Will Grow In Any Type Of Soil As Long As It Is Moist

Botanical Name	Common Name	Attributes	Height	Spread	Light Requirement	Drought Tolerance	USDA Hardiness Zones	AHS Heat Zones	Annual or Perennial
Osmunda cinnamomea	Cinnamon fern	Deciduous. Fuzzy, cinnamon colored fiddle-heads. Bronze fronds in fall	3–5 ft.	2–3 ft.	Shade with filtered sun	Low	2–10	9–1	P
Thelypteris kunthii	Southern shield fern	Deciduous. Soft, lime green fronds	2–4 ft.	1–4 ft.	Full sun or part shade	Low	7–11	9–1 (est.)	P

Plants With Interesting Foliage That Are Indifferent To Soils Types

Botanical Name	Common Name	Attributes	Height	Spread	Light Requirement	Drought Tolerance	USDA Hardiness Zones	AHS Heat Zones	Annual or Perennial
Zamia furfuracea	Cardboard palm	Interesting leaf shape	2–5 ft.	5–8 ft.	Sun or shade	High	(8)9–11	12–7 (est.)	P
Zamia intergrifolia	Florida arrowroot	Interesting leaf shape	1 1/2–2 1/2ft.	3 ft.	Full sun or part shade	High	8–11	12–7 (est.)	P

Plants with Interesting Foliage That Prefer Loamy to Sandy Soil

Botanical Name	Common Name	Attributes	Height	Spread	Light Requirement	Drought Tolerance	USDA Hardiness Zones	AHS Heat Zones	Annual or Perennial
Aspidistra elatior	Cast iron plant	Dark green leaf shape	2 1/2 ft.	2–3 ft. clumps	Shade	Moderate	7–11	Unknown	P
Aspidistra elatior 'Asahi'	Cast iron plant	Lighter green on tips or frosted effect	2 1/2 ft.	2–3 ft. clumps	Shade	Moderate	7–11	Unknown	P
Aspidistra elatior 'Dwarf Milky Way'	Cast iron plant	Flecked with yellow spots	1 1/2 ft.	1 1/2–2 ft. clumps	Shade	Moderate	7–11	Unknown	P
Aspidistra elatior Variegata	Cast iron plant	Creamy white vertical stripes	2 1/2 ft.	2–3 ft. clumps	Shade	Moderate	7–11	Unknown	P
Aspidistra elatior 'Milky Way'	Cast iron plant	Flecked with yellow spots	2 1/2 ft.	2–3 ft. clumps	Shade	Moderate	7–11	Unknown	P

Plants with Interesting Foliage That Prefer Loamy, Moist and Well-Drained Soils

Botanical Name	Common Name	Attributes	Height	Spread	Light Requirements	Drought Tolerance	USDA Hardiness Zones	AHS Heat Zones	Annual or Perennial
Cyrtomium falcatum (C. imbricatum)	Holly fern	Shiny, dark green, hollylike leaves	24–30 in.	30-in.	Shade with filtered sun	Low	6–10	12–7	P
Setcreasea pallida	Purple heart	Purple leaves	1–1 1/2 ft.	Indeterminate	Sun or shade	High	(7)8–11	12–1	P
Setcreasea pallida 'Kartzu Giant'	'Kartzu Giant' purple heart	Purple leaves	2 1/2–3 ft.	2-foot clumps	Sun or shade	High	7b–10	12–1	P
Setcreasea pallida 'Variegata'	Variegated purple heart	Pink and purple leaves	1–1 1/2 ft.	Indeterminate	Sun or shade	High	7–10	12–1	P
Strobilanthes dyeranus	Persian shield	Purple leaves	3–5 ft.	3 ft.	Full sun or part shade	None	9–11	Unknown	P
Strobilanthes dyeranus	Persian shield	Purple leaves	24–30 in.	3 ft.	Full sun or part shade	None	8	Unknown	A

Plants with Interesting Foliage Drought Tolerance Ratings

Botanical Name	Common Name	Soil Requirements	Drought Tolerance	USDA Hardiness Zones	AHS Heat Zones	Annual or Perennial
Setcreasea pallida	Purple heart	Moist and well-drained	High	(7)8–11	12–1	P
Setcreasea pallida 'Kartuz Giant'	'Kartuz Giant' purple heart	Moist and well-drained	High	7b–10	12–1	P
Setcreasea pallida 'Variegata'	Variegated purple heart	Moist and well-drained	High	7–10	12–1	P
Zamia furfuracea	Cardboard palm	Indifferent	High	(8)9–11	12–7 (est.)	P
Zamia intergrifolia	Florida arrowroot	Indifferent	High	8–11	12–7 (est.)	P
Aspidistra elatior	Cast iron plant	Loamy to sandy	Moderate	7–11	Unknown	P
Aspidistra elatior 'Asahi'	Cast iron plant	Loamy to sandy	Moderate	7–11	Unknown	P
Aspidistra elatior 'Dwarf Milky Way'	Cast iron plant	Loamy to sandy	Moderate	7–11	Unknown	P
Aspidistra elatior 'Variegata'	Cast iron plant	Loamy to sandy	Moderate	7–11	Unknown	P
Aspidistra elatior 'Milky Way'	Cast iron plant	Loamy to sandy	Moderate	7–11	Unknown	P
Cyrtomium falcatum (C. imbricatum)	Holly fern	Moist and loamy	Low	6–10	12–7	P
Osmunda cinnamomea	Cinnamon fern	Any type as long as it's moist	Low	2–10	9–1	P

Plants with Interesting Foliage Drought Tolerance Ratings (continued)

Botanical Name	Common Name	Soil Requirements	Drought Tolerance	USDA Hardiness Zones	AHS Heat Zones	Annual or Perennial
Thelypteris kunthii	Southern shield fern	Any type as long as it's moist	Low	7–11	9–1(est.)	P
Strobilanthes dyerianus	Persian shield	Well-drained, moist and loamy	None	9–11	Unknown	P
Strobilanthes dyerianus	Persian shield	Well-drained, moist and loamy	None	8	Unknown	A

Plants With Interesting Foliage That Are Evergreen

Botanical Name	Common Name
Aspidistra elatior 'Variegata'	Cast iron plant
Aspidistra elatior	Cast iron plant
Aspidistra elatior 'Dwarf Milky Way'	Cast iron plant
Aspidistra elatior 'Milky Way'	Cast iron plant
Zamia intergrifolia	Florida arrowroot
Zamia furfuracea	Cardboard palm
Aspidistra elatior 'Asahi'	Cast iron plant
Cyrtomium falcatum (C. imbricatum)	Holly fern

Plants with Interesting Foliage That Have Interesting Color Characteristics

Botanical Name	Common Name	Attributes
Osmunda cinnamomea	Cinnamon fern	Fuzzy, cinnamon colored fiddleheads. Bronze fronds in fall
Aspidistra elatior 'Variegata'	Cast iron plant	Creamy white vertical stripes
Aspidistra elatior 'Dwarf Milky Way'	Cast iron plant	Flecked with yellow spots
Aspidistra elatior 'Milky Way'	Cast iron plant	Flecked with yellow spots
Aspidistra elatior 'Asahi'	Cast iron plant	Lighter green on tips or frosted effect
Setcreasea pallida 'Variegata'	Variegated purple heart	Pink and purple leaves
Setcreasea pallida	Purple heart	Purple leaves
Setcreasea pallida 'Kartuz Giant'	'Kartuz Giant' purple heart	Purple leaves
Strobilanthes dyerianus	Persian shield	Purple leaves
Strobilanthes dyerianus	Persian shield	Purple leaves

Recommended Reading

Folks who have moved from colder climates to the Deep South are often at a loss when it comes to collecting gardening information. I suggest starting at the local library. Expect an exhilarating but overwhelming first visit. Don't panic. This is supposed to be fun. Keep reading and make a few notes in your gardening journal.

I also recommend contacting the nearest university extension service. All of the land grant universities have mostly free, printed information that is available from their county offices or from the Internet.

Recently graduated Master Gardeners often ask me what books are in my private collection. The following is a list of my personal favorites or ones that I consulted while writing this book.

Ackerson, Cornelius. *The Complete Book of Chrysanthemums.* New York: American Garden Guild, 1957.

It's too bad that no one has written a home gardening book about chrysanthemums for almost a half century. Fortunately, Mr. Ackerson's book is still available and his information continues to be timely.

Adams, Denise Wiles. *Restoring American Gardens: An Encyclopedia of Heirloom Ornamental Plants 1640–1940.* Portland, OR: Timber Press, 2004.

This book is a must for anyone who wants to cultivate a period garden or who is simply curious about historic landscapes.

Andrews, Jean. *Peppers: The Domesticated Capsicums, New Edition.* Austin: University of Texas Press, 1995.

No serious pepper aficionado should be without Jean Andrews or Dave DeWitt's books.

Armitage, Allan. *Armitage's Garden Annuals: A Color Encyclopedia.* Portland, OR: Timber Press, 2004.

Armitage, Allan. *Armitage's Manual of Annuals, Biennials, and Half-Hardy Perennials.* Portland, OR: Timber Press, 2001.

Barash, Cathy Wilkinson. *The Climbing Garden*. New York: Friedman/Fairfax Publishers, 2000.

Bender, Steve and Felder Rushing. *Passalong Plants*. Chapel Hill: University of North Carolina Press, 1993.

Burbank, Luther with Wilbur Hall. *The Harvest of the Years*. Honolulu, Hawaii: University Press of the Pacific, 2000.
I'm happy to see that Mr. Burbank's book is still available, although it is in paperback. For purists who prefer Houghton Mifflin Company's 1927 first edition in hardback, try finding it in used bookstores or purchase it from abe-books.com.

Cathey, H. Marc. *Heat-Zone Gardening: How to Choose Plants That Thrive in Your Region's Warmest Weather*. Alexandria, VA: Time-Life Books, 1998.

Chaplin, Lois Trigg. *A Southern Gardener's Book of Lists: The Best Plants For All Your Needs, Wants, and Whims*. Dallas: Taylor Publishing, 1994.

Crandall, Chuck and Barbara Crandall. *Flowering, Fruiting & Foliage Vines: A Gardener's Guide*. New York: Sterling Publishing Company, Inc., 1995.

DeWitt, Dave and Paul W. Bosland. *The Pepper Garden*. Berkeley, CA: Ten Speed Press, 1993.

Dunbar, Lin. *Ferns of the Coastal Plain: Their Lore, Legends and Uses*. Columbia, SC: University of South Carolina Press, 1989.

Garden Club of Charleston. *The Gardener's Guide to Charleston and the Lowcountry*. Charleston, SC: 1990.

Gartin, P.J. and F. Brian Smith. *Some Like It Hot: Plants That Thrive in Hot and Humid Weather*. Charleston, SC: Wyrick & Company, 2004.

Jefferson-Brown, Michael. *Ramblers Scramblers & Twiners: High-performance Climbing Plants & Wall Shrubs*. UK: David & Charles Brunel House, 1999.

Mitchell, Henry. *The Essential Earthman: Henry Mitchell on Gardening*. Boston: Houghton Mifflin Company, 1999.

Mitchell, Henry. *Henry Mitchell on Gardening*. Boston: Houghton Mifflin Company, 1998.

Mitchell, Henry. *One Man's Garden*. Boston: Houghton Mifflin Company, 1992.

Sullivan, Barbara. *Perennials for the Coastal South*. Chapel Hill: University of North Carolina Press, 2002.

Swain, Roger B. *The Practical Gardener: A Guide to Breaking New Ground*. Boston: Little, Brown and Company, 1989.
Although Roger Swain gardens up north, his science-based information is applicable anywhere. Read more than just his chapters titled "Sowing Seeds Indoors" and "Seedlings Under Light."

Trustees' Garden Club. *Garden Guide to the Lower South*, rev. ed. Savannah, GA: 1991.

Winterrowd, Wayne. *Annuals and Tender Plants for North American Gardens.* New York: Random House, 2004.

Whitelock, Loran M. *The Cycads.* Portland, OR: Timber Press, 2002.

Wyman, Donald. *Wyman's Gardening Encyclopedia.* New York: Scribner, 1986.

Suppliers
of Plants

With the exception of a few plants mentioned in this book, most can be found at
local garden centers. I highly recommend
starting with them first. If you cannot find
a particular plant, by all means ask if it
can be ordered. I have never been refused
a reasonable request.

Garden centers and seed catalogs also offer sterile potting mediums, rooting hormones, and heat coils for starting plants indoors. And to folks who enjoy propagation from cuttings, please ask before taking a piece of someone else's plant. I have found that most gardeners love to share, so I can't imagine a "May I please?" ever being turned down. In the event there is no one to ask, using sharp pruners instead of yanking and ripping is greatly appreciated. There is something reassuring about discovering a gently taken snip from your garden. It is like a whispered thank you.

I have found that many gardeners prefer to start seeds rather than purchase plants. The reasons are many, but color selection certainly tops the list. There are hundreds of reliable seed companies to choose from, but I have only included my tried and true trusted friends.

Retail Mail Order—Plants

Nurseries Caroliniana
22 Stephens Estate
North Augusta, SC 29860
803.279.2707
www.nurcar.com
Also wholesale

Plant Delights Nursery, Inc.
9241 Sauls Road.
Raleigh, NC 27603
www.plantdelights.com

Woodlanders
1128 Colleton Avenue
Aiken, SC 29801
803.648.7522
www.woodlanders.net

Stokes Tropical
4806 E Old Spanish Trail
Jeanerette, LA 70544
Order: 800.624.9706
Information: 337.365.6998
Fax: 337.365.6991
www.stokestropicals.com

Yucca Do Nursery
P.O. Box 907
Hempstead, Texas 77445
Telephone: 979.826.4580
Fax: 979.826.4571
www.yuccado.com

Singing Springs Nursery
8802 Wilkerson Road
Cedar Grove, NC 27231
Fax: 919.732.6336
Telephone: 919.732.9403
www.SingingSpringsNursery.com

Wholesale Only—Plants

Monrovia Growers
1833 E. Foothill Blvd.
Azusa, CA 91702-2638
Fax 626.334.3126
www.monrovia.com

Sandy Hill Plant Farm
P.O. Box 329
Mineola, TX 75773
Telephone: 903.569.6318
Fax: 903.569.0603
sandyhillplantfarm@earthlink.net

San Felasco
7315 N.W. 126th St.
Gainesville, Fl 32653
352.332.1220
www.sanfelasco.com

Retail Mail Order—Mostly Seeds

Thompson & Morgan Seedsmen, Inc.
P.O. Box 1308
Jackson, NH 08527-0308
Telephone: 800.274.7333
Fax 888.466.4769
www.thompson-morgan.com

Geo. W. Park Seed Co., Inc.
1 Parkton Ave.
Greenwood, SC 29647-0001
Telephone: 800.845.3369
Fax: 800.275.9941
www.parkseed.com

W. Atlee Burpee & Co.
Warminster, PA 18974
Telephone: 800.888.1447
Fax 800.487.5530
www.burpee.com

The Pepper Gal
P.O. Box 23006
Ft. Lauderdale, FL 33037-3006
www.peppergal.com

Whatcom Seed Company
P.O. Box 40700
Eugene, OR 97404
http://seedrack.com/

Index